THE MORMON CONCEPT OF GOD

A Philosophical Analysis

Francis J. Beckwith
and
Stephen E. Parrish

Studies in American Religion
Volume 55

The Edwin Mellen Press
Lewiston/Queenston/Lampeter

Library of Congress Cataloging in Publication Data

This volume has been registered with The Library of Congress.

This is volume 55 in the continuing series
Studies in American Religion
Volume 55 ISBN 0-7734-9787-0
SAR Series ISBN 0-88946-992-X

A CIP catalog record for this book
is available from the British Library.

The Edwin Mellen Press
Box 450
Lewiston, New York
USA 14092

The Edwin Mellen Press
Box 67
Queenston, Ontario
CANADA L0S 1L0

Edwin Mellen Press, Ltd.
Lampeter, Dyfed, Wales
UNITED KINGDOM SA48 7DY

Printed in the United States of America

DEDICATION

To my wife, Frankie
Francis J. Beckwith

To my wife, Sharon, and daughters, Sarah and Rebekah
Stephen E. Parrish

TABLE OF CONTENTS

ACKNOWLEDGEMENTS

We would like to thank the following individuals who read portions of this manuscript and offered valuable suggestions, although we take full responsibility for its contents: Dr. James A. Beckwith, Dr. J. David Turner (Professor of Communication Studies, Westmont College), Kevin Bywater, and Drs. Bruce Russell, Robert Yanal, and Lawrence Powers (Philosophy Department, Wayne State University), who were on Steve Parrish's master's thesis committee (Portions of this book are based on conclusions drawn in Steve's thesis). Special thanks to Christian Life Community Church of Las Vegas, Nevada, and its two pastors (David Walker and Ted Jeans) and secretary (Mary Lynn Biggs), who permitted us to use the church printer and computer for the final draft of this book. Frank Beckwith would like to thank his good friend Danny Green for a decade of encouragment and influence, which resulted in Frank's rigorous study of philosophy and alternative religious movements such as Mormonism. Without Danny, this book would have never been written. And finally, to W.R.M.: Well done, good and faithful servant.

Thanks to Bethany House Publishers for permission to use a chart from Bruce Tucker's, *Twisting the Truth* (Minneapolis: Bethany House, 1987), p. 148.

All Biblical references are taken from the *Jerusalem Bible* (Darton, Longman & Todd Ltd and Doubleday & Company, 1966, 1967 and 1968), unless otherwise indicated. Scripture quotations marked KJV are taken from the *King James Version*. Scripture quotations marked TEV are taken from *Today's English Version* (American Bible Society, 1966, 1976 and 1979).

INTRODUCTION

The Mormon concept of God is probably the most unique among American religious sects which claim to be Christian. Most traditional Christians who have written critical appraisals of Mormon theism have done so from a perspective best described as biblical. They have attempted to show why the Mormon concept of God is inconsistent with the concept of God which Christians have traditionally believed is portrayed in the Bible. Although this move has its theological merits, we believe that there are philosophical problems with the Mormon concept of God that have yet to be addressed by Christian philosophers. Furthermore, we know of no biblical critique of the Mormon concept of God that is adequate in showing why the classical view rather than the Mormon concept fits best with the biblical portrait of God.[1] The critiques which do exist nearly always *assume* that the classical view *is* the biblical view without defending this position with serious detail and/or rigor. For these reasons, the scope of this book is narrow, yet it ventures into uncharted territory. Our purpose is to show (1) that the Mormon concept of God differs radically from the classical concept of God, (2) that the Mormon concept of God contains many philosophical flaws, and (3) that the classical concept of God is more consistent with the Christian Scriptures than the Mormon view.

Although there are many Mormon philosophers and theologians who have philosophically criticized the classical concept of God, we will not deal with their objections in great detail in this text, since their critiques differ little from the many non-theistic critiques,[2] which we believe have been adequately dealt with in depth by a number of Christian philosophers and theologians.[3] But because of there obvious importance we certainly do not want to completely ignore these problems. For this reason, portions of our presentation of the classical view will deal with a few of the usual objections which are often echoed in Mormon philosophical literature.

The official name of the Mormon church is the Church of Jesus Christ of Latter-day Saints. It has its headquarters in Salt Lake City, Utah. Although there are many sects which call themselves Mormon,[4] this book's sole concern will be with the theology of the Salt Lake body, which is by far the largest of all the groups that claim to have their origin in the prophet Joseph Smith (1805-1844).[5]

Two years prior to his death, Smith explained how he became the founding prophet of this new religious body:

> I was at this time in my fifteenth year [spring 1820].... My mind at times was greatly excited, the cry and tumult were so great and incessant. The Presbyterians were most decided against the Baptists and Methodists, and used all the powers of both reason and sophistry to prove their errors.... On the other hand, the Baptists and Methodists in their turn were equally zealous in endeavoring to establish their own tenets and disprove all others.[6]

Because of these conflicting religious truth-claims, the adolescent Smith was confused as to which religion was correct. While reading the epistle of James, a particular passage seemed to point him in the right direction: "But if any of you lacks wisdom, he should pray to God, who will give it to him; because God gives generously and graciously to all." (James 1:5, TEV) Believing the passage was speaking personally to him, Smith retired to the woods so that he could be alone, kneel down and "ask of God." He writes of the circumstances which immediately followed the commencement of his request:

> I had scarcely done so, when immediately I was seized upon by some power which entirely overcame me, and had such an astonishing influence over me as to bind my tongue so that I could not speak. Thick darkness gathered round me, and it seemed to me for a time as if I were doomed to sudden destruction.....—just at this moment of great alarm, I saw a pillar of light exactly over my head, above the brightness of the sun, which descended gradually until it fell upon me.... When the light rested upon me I saw two Personages, whose brightness and glory defy all description, standing above me in the air. One of them spake unto me, calling me by name and said, pointing to the other—*This is My Beloved Son. Hear Him !*[7]

According to Smith, the two personages (God the Father and His Son Jesus Christ) told him to join none of the existing churches, "for they were all wrong." He was told that "their creeds were an abomination" and "that those professors were all corrupt." Smith claimed to have another startling vision on September 21, 1823, in which he was visited by the angel Moroni. The angel told Smith that there was buried on a nearby hill a book written upon golden plates. In order to help translate it correctly, special glasses (the Urim and Thumim) were placed with the plates. Four years after this vision (September 22, 1827), Moroni presented to Joseph the plates so that he can translate them. The translated plates are known today as the *Book of Mormon*, the alleged recording of God's relationship with peoples who at one time inhabited America. After the translation, the plates were given back to Moroni, and for this reason, they are incapable of being examined by trained archaeologists and linguists.[8]

Smith writes that on May 15, 1828 he and Oliver Cowdery were visited by John the Baptist who conferred upon them the Aaronic priesthood, *"which holds the keys of the ministering of angels and the gospel of repentance, and of baptism by immersion for the remission of sins."*[9] Soon afterwards (before the end of June, 1829) we are told that "Peter, James, and John had come and conferred upon Joseph and Oliver the keys of the Melchizedek Priesthood, the holy apostleship, by which authority they were authorized to organize the Church, ordain each other Elders, and also call and ordain others to the same office."[10] On April 6, 1830 Joseph Smith founded the "Church of Christ," which he later changed to its present name, the Church of Jesus Christ of Latter-day Saints. The Mormons claim that Smith was the vehicle God used to reinstate His true church which had vanished from the face of the earth soon after the deaths of Jesus' original apostles.

Despite major moves from Kirkland, Ohio to Jackson County, Missouri to Nauvoo, Mississippi, and finally to Salt Lake City, Utah (led by then president and successor to Smith, Brigham Young), the church's membership nevertheless increased in numbers. This is not to say that these moves spawned no schisms. A significant, although far from fatal, schism occurred a little over 15 years after Smith was gunned down in Carthage, Illinois (June 24, 1844), by a mob who attacked the jail in which he was placed after being summoned by legal authorities. Because they believed that the church should be ruled by direct descendants of Smith, the Reorganized Church of Jesus Christ of Latter-day Saints, which has its headquarters in Independence, Missouri, was formed in 1860.[11]

In addition to the *Book of Mormon*, Smith claimed to have received from God other revelatory works: the *Doctrine and Covenants* and *Pearl of Great Price*. Because most non-Mormons usually think of the *Book of Mormon* when they think of Mormonism, it comes as a surprise to them when they discover that it is really these latter two works, Smith's statements in his *History of the Church*, and the sayings and writings of the presidents of the church (who are thought to be divinely inspired successors of Smith) from which Mormonism derives most of the unique aspects of its view of God. Consequently, Mormonism is a religion, whose adherents claim is divinely inspired. But because the religion's alleged revelations have come down to us in a multiplicity of sources set forth in non-philosophical language, we shall attempt to explore the Mormon concept of God with care.

NOTES FOR INTRODUCTION

1. A rare exception to this is Robert A. Morey's *Battle of the Gods* (Southbridge, MA: Crown Publications, 1989), although Morey does not *specifically* critique the Mormon concept of God, but presents a general biblical critique of a finite god.

2. For example, see the articles by Kent E. Robson ("Omnipotence, Omnipresence, and Omniscience in Mormon Theology"), Blake T. Ostler ("The Concept of a Finite God as an Adequate Object of Worship"), and Peter C. Appleby ("Finitistic Theology and the Problem of Evil") in *Line Upon Line: Essays on Mormon Doctrine*, ed. Gary James Bergera (Salt Lake City, UT: Signature Books); Blake T. Ostler, "The Mormon Concept of God," *Dialogue: A Journal of Mormon Thought* 17 (Summer, 1984): 65-93; and David Lamont Paulsen, *The Comparative Coherency of Mormon (Finitistic) and Classical Theism* (Ann Arbor, MI: University Microfilms, 1975)

3. For example, see W. Norris Clarke, S.J., *The Philosophical Approach to God* (Winston-Salem, NC: Wake Forest University Press, 1979); Norman L. Geisler, "Process Theology," in *Tensions in Contemporary Theology*, eds. Stanley N. Gundry and Alan F. Johnson (Chicago: Moody Press, 1976), pp. 235-284; Thomas V. Morris, *The Logic of God Incarnate* (Ithaca, NY: Cornell University Press, 1986); Ronald H. Nash, *The Concept of God* (Grand Rapids, MI: Zondervan, 1983); Alvin Plantinga, *Does God Have a Nature?* (Milwaukee: Marquette University Press, 1980); Alvin Plantinga, *God, Freedom, and Evil* (Grand Rapids, MI: Eerdmans, 1974); and Richard Swinburne, *The Coherence of Theism* (Oxford: Clarendon, 1977)

4. See J. Gordon Melton, *An Encyclopedia of Cults in America* (New York: Garland, 1986), pp. 29-44; and Gordon H. Fraser, *Sects of the Latter-day Saints* (Eugene, OR: Industrial Litho, 1978).

5. As of 1982 the Utah Mormons had 5 million members (Rodney Clapp, "Fighting Mormonism in Utah," *Christianity Today* 26 [July 16, 1982]: 30). The second largest Mormon group, the Reorganized Church of Jesus Christ of Latter-day Saints, as of 1982 had 201,480 members and 1061 congregations. (J. Gordon Melton, *The Encyclopedia of American Religions*, 2nd ed. [Detroit, MI: Gale Research Company, 1987], pp. 710, 726-727).

6. "Joseph Smith, 2," from *The Pearl of Great Price*, 7, 9.

7. *Ibid.*, 15, 16.

8. *Ibid.*, 17-65. It is important to note that "before the plates were taken from earth, three witnesses prayed with Joseph that they might see them. An angel appeared and showed the plates individually so they could see the engravings on them. Their testimony about the plates is found in the front of *The Book of Mormon*. All three witnesses, Martin Harris, Oliver Cowdery and David Whitmer, left the LDS church. Harris came back in his old age, but Cowdery joined the Methodist church and before his death agreed with Whitmer that the LDS church was not God's true church. David Whitmer in *An Address to All Believers in Christ* (1887) claimed that Joseph Smith by 1833 had become a false prophet. However, he still maintained his testimony of the *Book of Mormon*. Eight others later also claimed to have witnessed the plates." (Donald S. Tingle, "Latter-day Saints (Mormons)," in *A Guide To Cults & New Religions*, ed. Ronald Enroth [Downers Grove, IL: InterVarsity, 1983], p. 119)

9. "Joseph Smith, 2," 69.

10. Joseph Smith, *History of the Church of Jesus Christ of Latter-Day Saints*, 7 vols., intro. and notes B.H. Roberts, 2nd ed. rev. (Salt Lake City: The Deseret Book Company, 1978), 1: 61. For brief summaries of the two Mormon priesthoods, see the appropriate articles in Bruce McConkie, *Mormon Doctrine*, 2nd ed. (Salt Lake City: Bookcraft, 1979)

11. For a brief history of the RLDS, see Melton, *Encyclopedia of Cults*, pp. 34-38.

1
THE CLASSICAL CONCEPT OF GOD

In order to better understand the Mormon concept of God, we believe that it is important that one understand the classical concept of God. Classical theism is the theism that has long been considered the orthodox theistic position of the Western World. It is the theism that is believed by most churches and religious bodies in the West, in particular the orthodox bodies that make up large segments of Christianity, Islam, and Judaism. Perhaps the most important distinguishing point about it is that it insists on God as infinite in all his attributes. The God of traditional theism can be described as (1) personal and disembodied, (2) the creator and sustainer of all contingent existence, (3) omnipotent, (4) omniscient, (5) omnipresent, (6) immutable, (7) the source of all values and perfectly good, (8) able to communicate with humans, and (9) necessary and the only God. Although all of these attributes have been criticized in one form or another sometime during the course of the history of philosophy, for our present purposes it will be necessary only to respond to the philosophical criticisms often voiced by Mormon philosophers which we believe if successful are sufficiently damaging to classical theism. For more detailed analyses of the classical attributes of God, we refer the reader to those works which we believe adequately deal in depth with these important issues (see note 3 on page 5).

PERSONAL AND DISEMBODIED

When the theist says that God is personal he means that God is a being who possesses rationality. That is to say, God is a being who is able to make decisions and act on them. God is a mind in the truest sense of the word. It is often said that God hears all our prayers. Sometimes he chooses to answer them, and sometimes he chooses not to answer them. In any event, such activity indicates rationality. Furthermore, traditional theism teaches that God loves and knows. Non-personal entities cannot love or know. Hence, God is a personal being.

The classical God is also disembodied. Unlike mortal human persons who possess bodies, there is no one physical entity to which the person of God is *uniquely* associated, although He has the ability to immediately control anything in the physical universe He so chooses. For this reason, God is also called a Spirit. Some of the objections that are raised by Mormon philosophers against the belief in God as Spirit will be discussed in our presentation of God as immutable and eternal.

THE CREATOR AND SUSTAINER OF ALL CONTINGENT EXISTENCE

The God of classical theism is that from which all contingent reality receives its existence in terms of both its origin and its continued existence. Unlike Plato's Demiurge who formed the universe out of pre-existent matter[1] or the God of Baha'ism who is co-eternal with the universe and from whom the universe emanates,[2] the God of classical theism created the universe *ex nihilo*, out of nothing. Everything in the universe is contingent upon and receives its existence from this being.

Mormon philosopher Blake Ostler has argued that the classical concept of creation is inconsistent with the classical concept of God being self-sufficient. Employing an argument originally developed by A.E. Taylor, Ostler writes:

> 1. If God possesses aseity [self-existence] and exists, then he is not dependent on anything nor lacking in any conceivable manner (i.e., God is self-sufficient).
> 2. A self-sufficient being cannot manifest a need nor be enhanced by any action (1).
> 3. Every positive action requires an explanation sufficient to account for it (Criteria of Sufficient Reason).
> 4. Creation of the cosmos is a positive action.

5. A self-sufficient being could not manifest a reason sufficient to explain why it preferred existence of the cosmos to its nonex-
istence (1,2).
6. Hence, God did not create the cosmos (3,4,5).[3]

In simple terms this argument is claiming that since any sufficient
reason for an act involves self-enhancement, God's act of creation involves
self-enhancement. But since God is self-sufficient, He does not need self-
enhancement. Therefore, if God created, He is not self-sufficient, and if God
is self-sufficient, He cannot create. We believe, however, that there is a
fundamental problem with this argument's use of the terms "self-sufficient"
and "sufficient reason." It seems that Ostler is confusing the "sufficient" in
self-sufficient with the "sufficient" in sufficient reason. The term *self-sufficient*, when describing the classical God, simply means that God is not
dependent on anything else for His being God; the reason for God's existence is within Himself, for He is what most theists call a Necessary Being, a
being who exists in every possible world (see below for a presentation of this
view). In traditional logic the term *sufficient* reason simply refers to a reason
which is enough for something else to be true, e.g., to be a citizen of Detroit
is sufficient to be a citizen of the state of Michigan. Hence, "sufficient" has
two different meanings in this argument.

Now if Ostler were to say that God is self-sufficient in the sense just
defined, it follows only that God cannot perform an act which *fulfills a lack*
in His nature (precisely because He lacks nothing), not that He cannot
perform any act for which He has sufficient reason to perform (as just defined). For this reason, it seems perfectly plausible to say that God's sufficient reason to create the universe is simply that he desired to do so for His
own pleasure although if He had created nothing whatsoever He would have
not ceased possessing the attributes of God, which is all that the classical
concept of self-sufficiency entails. Even if we do not know precisely *why*
God created the universe (i.e., God's *final* or *teleological* cause), it still does
not follow that He had to create in order to enhance His attributes. In fact, if
one could show *that* a *personal* God created the universe (i.e., that a person
is the universe's *efficient* cause), that the universe has not always existed, and
that the efficient cause of the universe is self-sufficient,[4] it would follow that
the efficient cause must have a purposeful reason for bringing the universe
into existence, whether or not we know of the reason. For the universe
would be co-eternal and one with God if the universe's existence is a neces-

sary condition for the enhancement of His attributes (but this is impossible, since a self-sufficient being does not *need* the universe), and a self-sufficient being is by definition a non-capricious being (i.e., a capricious being would lack rationality, and hence would not be self-sufficient).

OMNIPOTENT

God is also said to be all-powerful. To put it another way, God has the ability to do everything. But this must be qualified by saying that God can do anything that is (1) logically possible and (2) is consistent with him being a wholly perfect, personal, disembodied, omniscient, immutable, and necessary creator. These attributes should not be thought of as actually *limiting* God's power in a real sense, but rather they should be thought of as *perfections*, attributes at their infinitely highest level, which are essential to God's nature. Hence, it is not correct to say that they count against God's omnipotence. For example, because God is perfect, he is incapable of sinning; because he is personal, he cannot make himself impersonal; because he is omniscient (all-knowing) He is incapable of forgetting. This is consistent with the biblical portrayal of God being incapable of sinning (Mark 10:18, Hebrews 6:18), ceasing to exist (Exodus 3:14, Malachi 3:6), or not knowing something (Job 28:24, Psalm 139:17-18, Isaiah 46:10a).

What most classical theists mean by (1)—that God can do only that which is logically possible—can best be explained in answering a very popular challenge to God's omnipotence. It goes something like this: "If God is all-powerful, can He make a rock so big that He cannot lift it?" This challenge is trying to show that an all-powerful God is an incoherent concept by putting the theist in what appears to be an irreconcilable dilemma: If God is all-powerful, He can do anything, but if He *can* make a rock so big He cannot lift it, He is not really all-powerful because He can't lift the rock; but if He *can't* make a rock so big that He cannot lift it, He is not all-powerful because He is incapable of creating such a big rock. Either way, God loses.

This dilemma can be resolved by pointing out that God can only do that which is *logically possible*. Examples of logically *im*possible entities include "married-bachelors," "square-circles," and "a brother who is an only child." But they are not *really* entities. They are merely contradictory terms that are strung together and appear to say *some thing*. Concurring with this view, contemporary British philosopher Richard Swinburne writes:

A logically impossible action is not an action. It is what is described by a form of words which purport to describe an action, but do not describe anything which is coherent to suppose could be done. It is no objection to A's [God's] omnipotence that he cannot make a square circle. This is because "making a square circle" does not describe anything which it is coherent to suppose could be done.[5]

The medieval philosopher Thomas Aquinas makes a similar point:

Therefore, everything that does not imply a contradiction in terms is numbered among these possibles in respect of which God is called omnipotent; whereas whatever implies contradiction does not come within the scope of divine omnipotence, because it cannot have the aspect of possibility. Hence it is more appropriate to say that such things cannot be done, than that God cannot do them. Nor is this contrary to the word of the angel, saying: *No word shall be impossible with God* (*Luke* i. 37). For whatever implies a contradiction cannot be a word, because no intellect can possibly conceive such a thing.[6]

Returning to our dilemma: Can God make a rock so big that He cannot lift it? The answer is no. To ask God to create an unliftable rock is to ask Him to do what is logically impossible. It would be like asking God to create a married bachelor or a square circle. That is to say, since an all-powerful being is, by definition, *unlimited* in His power, it is logically impossible for Him to be able to create something He is *unable* to lift, something that *exceeds* His unlimited power. For just as that which is round (a circle) cannot, by definition, have four equal sides (a square), that which is unlimited in power cannot, by definition, have its power exceeded. Does this make God less than omnipotent? Not at all. Although it is impossible for God to make a rock so big He cannot lift it, He *can* make the biggest rock possible and He *can* also lift it. In summary, William Rowe has correctly point out that when a theist says that God is omnipotent he is saying that "God can do anything that is an absolute possibility (i.e., logically possible) *and not inconsistent with any of his basic attributes*."[7]

OMNISCIENT

The classical theist believes that God is all-knowing, omniscient. According to philosopher Ronald Nash, "Divine omniscience means that God holds no false beliefs. Not only are all of God's beliefs true, the range of his knowledge is total; He knows all true propositions."[8] God's knowledge is of the *past*, *present*, and *future*. It also seems to follow that since God has no need for any sense apparatus (e.g., eye, ear, nose, etc.) by which to acquire knowledge because He has always possessed all-knowledge, God knows everything *immediately*; for if he knew things *mediately* (through some medium such as a sense organ), it would follow that at some moment prior to him acquiring a piece of knowledge there would have been a time at which God did not know something that had already happened.

Since some classical theists believe that human beings possess the free will to make alternative choices, some Mormon thinkers try to show that this concept of free-will is inconsistent with God's omniscience.[9] This is usually pointed out in the form of a question: "If God knows what will definitely happen in the future, how can I have free will?" This challenge can be better understood in the following example. Suppose that it is Tuesday and Pat is mowing his lawn. If God knows the future, then God knew from all eternity that Pat would definitely mow his lawn on Tuesday. But if God's knowledge is always true, then it would seem that Pat had no choice but to mow his lawn on Tuesday. For if Pat had changed his mind and decided not to mow his lawn, then God's knowledge would have been incorrect. But this is impossible, for God's knowledge is always true. Therefore, it seems that since Pat cannot refrain from mowing his lawn on Tuesday because God's knowledge is immutable, human free will and divine omniscience cannot exist at the same time. Either God knows the future and human beings are not free, or human beings are free and God does not know the future. This example can be presented in the following argument outline:

1. God's knowledge of the future is always true.
2. Therefore, God knows what will definitely happen.
3. "Pat will mow his lawn on Tuesday" is part of this definite future.
4. Free will is the ability to do otherwise.
5. Therefore, "Pat will mow his lawn on Tuesday" could not have been otherwise.
6. Therefore, God's omniscience eliminates human free will.

Let us examine each one of these premises and see why this argument is not a very good one. There is no dispute with premises one and two. It follows from God's omniscience that God knows what will definitely happen. Premises 3 and 4 seem to also to be uncontroversial for most theists.[10] However, it is with the fifth premise which we have a strong disagreement. For it does not seem to follow that because Pat's Tuesday lawn mowing is definite and free will involves the ability to do otherwise that Pat's Tuesday lawn mowing could not have been otherwise (i.e., this lawn-mowing would have not happened if Pat had chosen to do something different). The following example concerning the past should help make this easy to understand.

Suppose the following is true: "On July 12, 1986 Jim *definitely* married Kim." Although this *definitely* did happen, and therefore cannot be changed, this does not mean that neither Jim nor Kim were acting freely. Either one of them could have chosen to back out at the last moment, marry somebody else, postpone the wedding for another year or two, etc. However, as it turned out, they freely chose to marry each other instead of freely doing something else. The upshot of all this is that if one of them had decided to not get married to the other, then the *definite* past *would have been different*. Hence, the fact that a human action in the past definitely happened does not mean that it could not have been different or that human free will was not involved.

This is also true of the future. Returning to our initial example, if Pat had chosen *not* to mow his lawn on Tuesday, then God's knowledge *would have* been different. In other words, just because something definitely *will* happen does not mean that it *must* happen. God's knowledge of our future actions is brought about by the *free* actions we will perform in the future. God knows what will definitely happen because we will freely act in a certain way, not because we *must* act in a certain way. Hence, Ostler is wrong when he states that the omniscience/free will "issue is one of fatalism, the notion that future events are inevitable."[11] Christian philosopher William Lane Craig sums it rather well:

> From God's foreknowledge of a free action, one may infer only that the action will occur, not that it must occur. The agent performing the action has the power to refrain, and were the agent to do so, God's foreknowledge would have been different. Agents cannot bring it about both that God foreknows their action and that they do not perform the action, but this is no limitation on their freedom. They are free either to act or to refrain, and whichever they choose, God will have foreknown.[12]

How this view of omniscience and free-will ties in with God's immutability (i.e., unchangeableness) and eternal nature will be made clear when we deal with both those attributes below.

OMNIPRESENT

God's omnipresence is an attribute which logically follows from His omniscience, disembodiment, omnipotence, and role as sustainer and creator of the universe. That is to say, since God knows everything immediately without benefit of sensory organs, is not limited by any particular spatio-temporal body, and sustains the existence of the entire universe, it follows that God is in some sense present everywhere. We believe that Thomas Aquinas' position adequately clarifies this doctrine. Swinburne presents Aquinas' position:

> This doctrine has been expounded very clearly by Aquinas in *Summa Theologiae*, I.8, and I will outline briefly his exposition. God, writes Aquinas, exists everywhere in the first place because he acts everywhere. He does not act through intermediaries, but directly. He acts everywhere because he gives existence and power to things in all places. In Article 3 of the cited question Aquinas argues for the proposition that 'God is everywhere in substance, power, and presence'. 'God exists in everything by power inasmuch as everything is subject to his power, by presence inasmuch as everything is naked and open to his gaze, and by substance inasmuch as he exists in everything causing their existence.' God being everywhere by power and substance is thus a matter of all things being subject to his direct control. God being everywhere by presence is a matter of him knowing goings on everywhere, without being dependent for his knowledge on such intermediaries as eyes and ears.[13]

IMMUTABLE AND ETERNAL

When a theist claims that God is immutable, she is asserting that God is unchanging. God has always been God. There never was a time when God was not God. He did not become God by getting good grades at some cosmic "divinity school" or by "going through the ranks" or anything of that sort. God has been God for all eternity. His nature has always been the same. God, unlike a fine wine, does not get better as the years go by. He is the best, always has been the best, and always will be the best.

Some may argue that to say that God is unchanging conflicts with the Christian affirmation that God has acted, and continues to act, in history. This objection can be put forth in the form of two questions: "If God is a personal God Who reveals Himself in history—interacting in the lives of men and women—does He change in relation to the needs and desires of His creatures? If so, how can this be reconciled with the doctrine of immutability?" We believe that the best way to respond to this problem is to clarify what Christian theists mean when they speak of immutability. We believe that it is correct to say that when theists speak of immutability, they do not mean a static view of unchangeability (that is, God is simply an eternally inactive being). Rather, they hold to a view which retains the relational aspect of God's nature (i.e., His interaction with His creatures) without compromising His immutability. The following example should help explain this view.

In the book of Jonah, God made a contingent promise to the city of Ninevah. He said that if Ninevah did not repent and turn from its wicked ways, He would destroy the city. As it turned out, the city of Ninevah repented and turned from its wicked ways and was spared the wrath of God. Although it appears that God "changed" in His attitude toward Ninevah from wrath to blessing, it is more accurate to say that the change occurred in the hearts and minds of the citizens of Ninevah; God remained the same. He did not change morally. He acted in accordance with His own immutable nature. Because He punishes wickedness and rewards righteousness on the basis of His moral nature, it can be said in the case of Ninevah that God retained his immutable nature and yet responded to the repentant hearts of His creatures. God did not change; Ninevah did.

Professor W. Norris Clarke writes that God's "*personal* immutability includes relational mutability." In other words, "the immutability attributed to God must be that proper to a perfect personal being—i.e., an *immutable intention* to love and save us, which intention then includes all the adaptations and responses necessary to carry this intention through in personal dialogue with us."[14] According to Clarke, God's

> consciousness is contingently and qualitatively *different* because of what we do. All this difference remains, however, on the level of God's *relational consciousness* and therefore does not involve increase or decrease in the Infinite Plenitude of God's *intrinsic inner being* and perfection.... God does not become a more or less perfect being because of the love we return to Him and the joy He experiences thereat (or its absence).[15]

In light of the Ninevah example, Clarke is saying that God's *relational consciousness* changed when Ninevah repented—i.e., God chose not to destroy the city—but His *intrinsic inner being* remained constant and immutable (in this case, the moral aspect of His nature). Hence, the change in God's relational consciousness is such that it functions in accordance with his immutable intrinsic inner being. In this sense, God is immutable.

God's immutability often brings up the question of whether or not God exists in or out of time. Classical theists, for the most part, have defended God's timelessness. They refer to God as *eternal*. Although God does act *in time*, he is not bound by time, and hence transcends it. If He is the Creator and Sustainer of all that exists, including both space and time, as traditional theists have often argued, it follows that God is not restricted or limited by time. In this sense He is timeless.

How does this view of timelessness fit in with our view of God's relational consciousness and intrinsic inner being? We believe that the following is a philosophical model which best answers this question. Logically prior to creating this world (i.e., the world we live in), W, God could have created a number of different worlds—W_1, W_2, W_3... W_n—with different futures in which the creatures in those worlds choose freely to act in certain ways to which God either chooses or does not choose to respond. And in line with our discussion of omniscience, it makes perfect sense to assert that God eternally knows how people will freely act in the future of the world He freely chooses to create. Hence, neither the existence of any one of those worlds nor the free actions of any of its creatures is part of God's intrinsic inner being. That is, God's relational consciousness could be different depending on which world He creates and how those creatures freely choose to act in that world, but His intrinsic inner being remains the same. For example, God eternally (timelessly) thinks that Steve P., a creature in actual world W, writes a letter on June 6, 1989, but had God created a different world, such as W_1, in which Steve P. never existed, or had Steve P. chosen not to write a letter in W, then God's relational consciousness would have been eternally different. In the case of Ninevah, God eternally knows that if He creates W, Ninevah can either choose or not choose to repent. And God eternally knows that in W the Ninevites will choose to repent and He responds accordingly, and He eternally knows which we way He will respond. Of course, God would have destroyed them had they freely chosen not to repent. In any event, classical theists have defended a view of immutability which entails the view that God is timeless, which they believe when properly clarified is not inconsistent with Him acting in time. Hence, what we have covered thus far, both in our current discussion and in the previous sections on omniscience and creation, seems to refute Ostler's contention that "a timeless being.... could not coherently do any of the things the biblical deity is said to have done, such as create a world, enter into a relationship with a human being, or respond in prayer."[16]

However, two more of Ostler's objections must be dealt with. The first goes something like this: a timeless God cannot possess such distinctively human attributes as the ability to care, judge, forgive, etc., "for all of these actions logically entail a succession in time."[17]

The problem with this objection is that it confuses God's personal activity *in time* with His immutable essence which transcends time and space. That is, classical theism teaches that God reveals His love, care, forgiveness, and judgment by personally interacting with us in time, but His essence or nature is not limited by time. In light of the clarifications we have made concerning immutability, omniscience, free-will, and creation (see above), it is perfectly coherent to say that "God acts from eternity but the results are in time."[18] Hence, God's personal interaction with His creatures occurs in a succession in time, although He has willed this interaction from all eternity, contingent upon the world He chooses to create and how the creatures in that world will freely choose. This means that our actions make a difference to God and in eternity, that our prayers and petitions do count, and that the classical concept of God is consistent with these notions. Of course, God does not possess in a fully human sense what Ostler calls "human attributes," but this does not mean that God does not possess the same attributes in an infinite sense or that He cannot exercise these unchanging attributes in time and in relationship with His creation, which seems to follow from the concept of an Infinite God Who is *Personal* but not essentially human.

Ostler's second objection asks the question: Is it coherent to suppose that a disembodied personal entity (i.e., a spirit) can really be timeless? He writes:

> I believe that the idea of a God who is in no place and in no time is an idea of no God. If God is incorporeal in the sense that he lacks all spatial extension, then he lacks temporal identity. He cannot consistently be conceived as a personal identity because he lacks all criteria of identity. There is no way to distinguish him from any other entity. If God does not have temporal or "bodily" extension, *person* has no cognitive content when applied to him.[19]

Ostler is simply arguing that if one conceives of God as an incorporeal entity who lacks all spatial extension (that is, He is not limited by space and time), then God also lacks temporal identity and personal identity, since to be conceived as personal identity one must have spatial extension. There are at least four problems with this argument. First, it is clearly circular. For we are told that the reason why God cannot be personal is because he lacks spatial extension which is a necessary condition for temporal identity and temporal identity is a necessary condition for personal identity. But then we are told that the reason why one must have temporal identity in order to have personal identity is because without "bodily" extension (that is, temporal identity) "*person* has no cognitive content when applied to him [God]." Ostler's argument is similar to the one put forth by the zealous political science professor who asserted that "democracy is the best form of government because there is no better government than one run by the people." Hence, Ostler has not sufficiently demonstrated why bodily extension is a necessary condition for personal identity.

Second, by not considering the full nature of the classical God, Ostler draws the mistaken inference that because God does not have bodily extension one cannot distinguish Him from any other entity. There is no doubt that the identity of disembodied persons in general is problematic, although we believe that philosophers have adequately responded to these objections.[20] We are, however, concerned with a disembodied *God*, a self-existent disembodied personal creator of the universe. With this in mind, Ostler's objection seems most unusual. For it seems perfectly plausible to say that a self-existent disembodied personal creator of everything should have no problem with providing His creatures with an intuitive mechanism by which to identify Him on certain occasions. This is no desperate theory in order to rescue the classical God (i.e., an *ad hoc* hypothesis), since God's ability to grant such an intuition to His creatures follows logically from His omnipotence.

Third, when one asserts that personal identity logically depends on physical reality, one assumes a dubious worldview. This worldview is known as *physicalism*, which "holds that everything that exists is nothing but a spatio-temporal system which can be completely described in terms of some ideal form of physics."[21] But if this is true, then all our thought processes are the result of the non-rational natural mechanism of the physical universe. And if non-rational forces are responsible for our thoughts, then there is no reason to trust our thinking. Hence, there is no reason to believe that physicalism is true. J.P. Moreland point out a number of philosophical problems with physicalism,[22] not the least of which is its self-refuting nature:

> When a statement fails to satisfy itself (i.e., to conform to its own criteria of validity or acceptability), it is self-refuting.... Consider some examples. "I cannot say a word of English" is self-refuting when uttered in English. "I do not exist" is self-refuting, for one must exist to utter it. The claim "there are no truths" is self-refuting. If it is false, then it is false. But if it is true, then it is false as well, for in that case there would be no truths, including the statement itself.[23]

In sum, it is self-refuting to *argue* that one *ought* to *choose* physicalism *because* he should *see* that the *evidence* is *good* for physicalism. Physicalism cannot be offered as a rational theory because physicalism does away with the necessary preconditions for there to be such a thing as rationality. Physicalism usually denies intentionality by reducing it to a physical relation of input/output, thereby denying that the mind is genuinely capable of having thoughts *about* the world. Physicalism denies the existence of propositions and nonphysical laws of logic and evidence which can be in minds and influence thinking. Physicalism denies the existence of a faculty capable of rational insight into these nonphysical laws and propositions, and it denies the existence of an enduring "I" which is present through the process of reflection. Finally, it denies the existence of a genuine agent who deliberates and chooses positions because they are rational, an act possible only if physical factors are not sufficient for determining future behavior.[24]

Therefore, the Mormon metaphysical worldview of physicalism, which grounds Ostler's notion of personal identity as dependent on bodily extension, is clearly self-refuting or at least not necessarily true. And since mental realities cannot be sufficiently accounted for by appealing to matter,[25] it seems perfectly reasonable to believe that there could exist a Mind Who is disembodied.

And fourth, if there is an argument whose chief premises could be true (i.e., there is in principle nothing irrational in asserting them as in the case of "John is a married bachelor"), and which logically lead one to the conclusion that a disembodied timeless being exists, then it logically follows that there is no way in principle to dispense with the possibility that a disembodied timeless person exists. Consider the following argument:[26]

1. Everything that begins to exist does so only through a cause.
2. The universe had a beginning.
3. Therefore, the universe has a cause.
4. There cannot exist an infinite regress of causes in time.
5. Therefore, the cause of the universe is eternal and uncaused, from which we can infer particular attributes.

It is not important that we defend each one of these premises or that they be universally held truths, although both authors hold to the soundness of this argument. It is only important that we see that given the *possibility* of the truth of the premises, it is possible that a disembodied timeless person exists, which is all that is necessary to show that it is not *logically* incoherent to believe in the existence of such a being.

Premise one—that everything that begins to exist does so only through a cause—is certainly not impossible, as evidenced by the number of philosophers[27] and ordinary people who have defended and assumed its truth. Premise two—that the universe had a beginning—although somewhat more controversial than premise one, does not seem logically impossible. For the big bang theory of the origin of the cosmos is consistent with it,[28] in addition to being defended by philosophical argument in numerous works.[29] Furthermore, those who argue against the beginning of the universe do not do so on the basis of it being logically impossible, rather they try to show that the arguments of its defenders are not logically compelling.[30] Premise three is a conclusion and follows logically from premises one and two. Premise four—that there cannot exist an infinite regress of causes in time—although not considered true by some,[31] its logical possibility is never questioned. For it is certainly not logically incoherent to assert that the regress of causes in time is finite. And finally, if an infinite regress is impossible, then the final conclusion follows: there must exist a first cause which is eternal and uncaused.

We can infer at least three attributes from this conclusion. (1) The first cause was at least timeless prior to creation. William Lane Craig writes:

> Prior to creation, there was no time at all, for time cannot exist unless there is change. God Himself is changeless; otherwise you would find an infinite series of past events in His life, and we know that such an infinite series is impossible. So God is changeless, and hence, timeless prior to creation.[32]

Since it is coherent to speak of a first cause as timeless prior to creation, it seems that there is nothing incoherent in saying that there currently exists a timeless being.

(2) This first cause is disembodied. Since physical reality began with the beginning of the universe, and it is coherent to say that the first cause of the universe is timeless and eternal, it makes perfect sense to say that the first cause does not have a physical body. Granted we may have no idea *exactly* of what this first cause consists, we certainly know that it is not physical. And since we do have some notion of what a non-physical reality may be like (e.g., numbers, mental activity, and concepts are non-physical realities), it is not incoherent to assert that there can be a being which is disembodied.

(3) This first cause is personal. If all the conditions for the existence of the universe were present from all eternity, then the universe would be as eternal as its cause. But if the universe began to exist, then some condition

for its coming into existence was present at that moment which was not present for all eternity prior. Moreland explains that the only way to resolve this problem is to think of the first cause as personal or rational:

> If the necessary and sufficient conditions for a match to light are present, the match lights spontaneously. There is no deliberation, no waiting. In such situations, when A is the efficient cause of B, spontaneous change or mutability is built into the situation itself.
>
> The only way for the first event to arise spontaneously from a timeless, changeless, spaceless state of affairs, and at the same time be caused, is this—the event resulted from the free act of a person or agent. In the world, persons or agents spontaneously act to bring about events. I myself raise my arm when it is done deliberately. There may be necessary conditions for me to do this (e.g., I have a normal arm, I am not tied down), but these are not sufficient. The event is realized only when I freely act. Similarly, the first event came about when an agent freely chose to bring it about, and this choice was not the result of other conditions which were sufficient for that event to come about.[33]

Therefore, it seems perfectly reasonable to infer that the first cause of the universe is a personal being. Hence, since its premises are logically possible, this entire argument shows that the notion of a disembodied eternal person is not *a priori* irrational.

In sum, it seems that the concept of God as a timeless disembodied person cannot be discounted on the basis of Ostler's argument that personal identity is dependent on temporal and bodily extension. For we saw that this argument (1) is question-begging, (2) fails to take into consideration the classical God's ability to make His identity plain to His creation, (3) assumes the dubious worldview of physicalism, and (4) ignores an argument whose logically possible premises show that one cannot dispense with a disembodied eternal person *a priori*.

We should make mention of the fact that there are some theists, who claim to be in the classical tradition, who argue that God is *everlasting*, that He has always existed but has done so *in time*.[34] We do not believe, however, that this position is as consistent with the Biblical data as the timelessness view (see chapter 5).

THE SOURCE OF ALL VALUES AND PERFECTLY GOOD

In classical theism God is not subject to a moral order outside of Himself. Neither are God's moral commands and value judgments completely arbitrary. The source of all values is God's own nature. In this way, theism does not fall prey to the Euthyphro dilemma, a dilemma put forth by Socrates in Plato's dialogue of the same name: "Is the pious loved by the gods because it is pious, or is it pious because it is loved by the gods?"[35] Nevertheless, some non-theists, such as Bertrand Russell,[36] have applied this to classical theism and have used it as a so-called moral disproof of God. Norman Geisler and Winfried Corduan outline Russell's argument:[37]

> 1. If there is a moral law, either it results from God's fiat or it does not.
> 2. If it results from God's fiat, it is arbitrary (and then God is not essentially good).
> 3. If it does not result from God's fiat, God too is subject to it (and if God is subject to it, then God is not ultimate; the moral law is).
> 4. So, either God is not essentially good (because he is arbitrary about what is right and wrong) or else God is not ultimate (because there is a moral law to which even he is subject).
> 5. But neither an arbitrary God nor a less than ultimate God is worthy of an ultimate commitment (i.e., neither is religiously worthy).
> 6. Therefore, there is no God (who is worthy of religious devotion).

One can see how this dilemma vanishes once one views God as the source of all values. Hence, Russell's application of the Euthyphro dilemma commits the fallacy of false alternatives, a fallacy which occurs when one mistakenly argues that there are only two choices in a matter (e.g., "Either you're a good student or a good athlete." Why can't you be both?). We agree with Geisler and Corduan (following in the tradition of Thomas Aquinas): "The moral law flows from the nature of God by way of the will of God. God's will is subject to God's nature, which nature is the basis for the moral law. And God is subject to his own nature."[38]

There is yet another reason to reject Russell's dilemma. Although we have yet to discuss the classical view that God exists in every possible world (that is, He has transworld existence), we will make mention here why this view eliminates the possibility that God's moral law is arbitrary. (This will be better understood after reading the section in this chapter on God's necessary existence.) For if God exists in all possible worlds (a possible world is simply a world that *could have been*, such as one in which Michael Dukakis defeats George Bush in 1988) and hence has the same values in all possible worlds, then God would will the same moral law in all possible worlds. And how can something that exists in and is the same in all possible worlds be arbitrary? Arbitrariness presupposes capriciousness and lack of rational justification. A moral law that flows from a being whose values exist necessarily in every possible world is hardly arbitrary. Furthermore, it follows from God being the source of all values that He is perfectly good.

ABLE TO COMMUNICATE WITH HUMANS

Traditional theists also believe that God is able to communicate with humans. Since God is a rational being, the ability to communicate seems to follow logically. Theists believe that God can communicate in many ways, although the authors of this work believe in *sola scriptura*, each defining this Protestant Reformed view a bit differently. Stephen E. Parrish defines *sola scriptura* to mean that besides the Bible there is no other propositional revelation. He argues that this was the position of the Reformers. On the other hand, Francis J. Beckwith defines the doctrine to mean that any alleged communication from God must be tested by the Bible. In any event, both authors believe that through the Bible God communicates certain truths about morality, salvation, human nature, divine nature, history, etc, which cannot be obtained through human reason alone.

Other ways in which theists have claimed that God communicates include the following, which are not necessarily accepted by the authors. First, some theists believe that God communicates through certain holy individuals. Orthodox Judaism believes that God has spoken through his prophets, such as Moses and Isaiah. Christians believe that Jesus of Nazareth, the Incarnate Son of God, was the ultimate in divine communication to humanity. Roman Catholic Christians believe that God communicates and gives direction to His people today through the Pope and hierarchy of His Church. Second, many theists believe that God communicates through certain "coincidental" circumstances and events. For example, some people "see" a message from God for their lives in a highly unlikely event, such as a phone call of acceptance from an employer moments after the theist had prayed for direction in finding a job. Third, some theists believe that God communicates through the miraculous, events that seem to violate scientific law and have a certain timing and awe-inspiring nature (e.g., a resurrection, a sudden inexplicable healing, etc. after an individual invokes the name of a certain God and stakes his theological claims on the actuality of the

miracle's occurrence).[39] Fourth, a number of theists believe that God sometimes communicates in contemporary times through the gift of prophecy.[40]
That is, some believers are blessed with the gift of telling their brethren
God's will for their lives and what sorts of circumstances await them in the
future. Fifth, there are some theists, although a very tiny number, who claim
God has spoken to them with an audible voice. Sixth, some theists have
argued that God has communicated his existence and attributes to humans
through the facts of nature. For example, it is sometimes claimed that the
intricacies and design of nature communicate to humans that there exists an
Infinite Designer of all that exists. This seems to be what the Apostle Paul is
saying when he writes: "For what can be known about God is perfectly plain
to them since God himself has made it plain. Ever since God created the
world his everlasting power and deity—however invisible—have been there
for the mind to see in the things he has made. That is why such people are
without excuse." (Romans 1:19-20) This is called natural theology.

The above does not pretend to be an exhaustive list of all the ways
theists have claimed that God has communicated. It would be wrong,
however, to ignore the fact that most theists believe that the communication
between God and humans is two-way. That is, human persons can communicate with God through such activities as worship, singing, and petitionary
prayer.[41]

NECESSARY AND THE ONLY GOD

Classical theism teaches that God is a Necessary Being, although
what is meant by this is not unanimously agreed upon by theists.[42] For instance, Swinburne lists six possible ways that the word "necessary" can be
defined in terms of God's existence.[43] We believe that the best way to define
God's necessity is in terms of *logical* necessity. What we mean by this will be
made clear in the following paragraphs.

God, according to the classical theist, is a being of which no greater
can be conceived. St. Anselm, who lived in the twelfth century, was one
philosopher who used this definition of God in the development of his
Ontological Argument.[44] Alvin Plantinga, in his discussion of the same
argument, uses a similar definition of God: "a being that has maximal greatness."[45] He writes:

> Necessarily, a being is maximally great only if it has maximal excellence in every world.

and

> Necessarily, a being has maximal excellence in every world only if it has omniscience, omnipotence, and moral perfection in every world.[46]

For Plantinga, a *possible world* is any imaginary world that *could have been* and is therefore logically possible. For example, in some possible world Michael Dukakis defeats George Bush for the 1988 presidential election, but in another possible world neither Bush nor Dukakis exists. There are possible worlds in which Bob Dylan can sing on key or not exist at all. Hence, when Plantinga says that God can be maximally great only if He has maximal excellence in every (possible) world, he means that unlike Dukakis, Bush, Dylan, and the rest of us, God *must* have maximal excellence, and hence exist, in every possible world. For if He did not exist and have maximal excellence in every possible world, then He would not be defined as possessing maximal greatness, since it is possible that another being (who possesses the attributes of God) could exist in every possible world and would be for this reason greater.

As we noted above, this definition of maximal greatness is close to Anselm's. For maximal greatness and excellence are identical to the idea of a being of which no greater can be conceived. Not only that, but the attributes that Plantinga gives to God are ones that Anselm and indeed almost all classical theists ascribe to Him. Also, the notion of God being the maximally greatest being implies, as Plantinga says, that he exists in all possible worlds. A being that exists in all possible worlds is certainly a *necessary* being; He is a being who can not *not* exist. This kind of necessity is called *logical* necessity. Just as it is logically necessary that a man who is unmarried be a bachelor or that a square be a geometric figure with four equal sides, it is logically necessary that the maximally greatest being have maximal excellence, and hence exist, in every possible world. But there is another concept of necessity proposed by some theists. This is the concept of *factual* necessity.

There has been a debate as to which concept of necessity is best, factual or logical. Many philosophers have rejected the ideal of a logically necessary being and have proposed as an alternative a factually necessary one. William Lane Craig states, "Although some philosophers still want to defend the notion of a logically necessary being, most prefer to speak of a factually necessary being."[47] A factually necessary being would be a being that would not exist out of logical necessity. He would not exist in every possible world. However, if He did exist, He could not pass out of existence. He would be an uncaused, indestructible, independent being. This stands in contrast to the logically necessary being who has the same attributes, and therefore exists, in every possible world.

As Craig indicates, most philosophers have moved from defending a logically necessary to a factually necessary being. However, there is some indication that philosophers are coming back to the concept of a logically necessary being. Be that as it may, it is logical necessity that we will defend. One reason is that factual necessity may imply logical necessity. Samuel Clarke thought so. He thought that the idea of a factually necessary or independent being naturally implied the idea of a logically necessary being. A factually necessary being would have to be of course, an independent being, because it would be uncaused and indestructible. To quote Clarke:

> ...the only idea of a self-existent or necessarily existing being, is the idea of a being the supposition of whose non-existing is an express contradiction. For since it is absolutely impossible but there must be somewhat self-existent; that is, which exists by the necessity of its own nature; it is plain that necessity cannot be a necessity consequent upon any foregoing supposition, (because nothing can be antecedent to that which is self-existence,) but it must be a necessity absolutely such in its own nature. Now a necessity, not relatively or consequently, but absolutely such in its own nature; is nothing else, but its being a plain impossibility or implying a contradiction to suppose the contrary. For instance, the relation of equality between twice two and four, is an absolute necessity; only because it is an immediate contradiction in terms to suppose them unequal. This is the only idea we can frame, of an absolute necessity; and to use the word in any other sense, seems to be using it without any signification at all.[48]

What Clarke is saying is that a being that exists by the necessity of its own nature cannot, by definition, be dependent on anything else for its existence, non-existence, or its attributes. And since it has the reason for its own existence in itself, it is unaffected (in terms of its own existence and nature) by anything extrinsic to itself. But in that case it would exist regardless of what the rest of the universe is like. Or in short, the necessary being would exist in all possible worlds. And a being that exists in all possible worlds is a logically necessary being. As William Rowe puts it, somewhat differently:

> But a being has the reason for its existence within its own nature only if it exists in every possible world. And clearly if any being exists in every possible world then that being is such that its non-existence is absolutely impossible.[49]

And a being whose non-existence is absolutely impossible is a being whose existence is logically necessary. Thus, it may be that the concept of a merely factually necessary being is a problematic one. As Ronald H. Nash writes:

> While the notion of God as a logically necessary being is once again becoming respectable, new doubts are being raised about the cogency of the concept of a factually necessary being. By definition, a factually necessary being does not exist in all possible worlds. (Only a logically necessary being could exist in every possible world.) Once one recognizes, however, that there are possible worlds in which a factually necessary God does not exist, it makes sense to ask why he exists in the *real* world. But the whole point to talking about a necessary being is supposedly to defuse questions like this. The advocate of factual necessity falls into a trap of his own making. The question as to why God exists in any particular world cannot possibly arise is the case of a logically necessary God. He exists in world *A* or *B* (and so on) because He exists in every possible world. But once a theist acknowledges that there are possible worlds in which God does not exist, the question as to why God exists in the real world gains force. Moreover, what prevents this factually necessary being from existing by chance, that is, without reason?
>
> It appears, then, that the notion of factual necessity appeals implicitly to key features of the concept of logical necessity. Either a necessary being exists in every possible world or it does not. A logically necessary being does exist in every possible world. In this sense, it is like the number two or the concept of square. To question *why* a necessary being exists in the real world makes no sense at all.[50]

Or in other words, a factually necessary being does not have to exist, and in that case it makes sense to ask why He exists. But the factually necessary God is supposed to be uncaused, indestructible, and independent of all other beings. Why then, does He exist, if nothing else can cause Him to be? He cannot be the cause of Himself, for the notion of a self-caused being is incoherent (This would imply that a non-existent being caused its own existence, which is absurd), just as it is incoherent to suppose that a son can be his own father. Since He is not caused by others or by Himself, He must be an uncaused being. Unlike the concept of the logically necessary being, however, it does make sense to ask why He exists. And since He is uncaused, and does not have the reason for His existence in Himself, unlike a logically necessary being, the only answer as to why He exists is that there is no answer. He exists for no reason. He exists by chance alone.

But a being that exists only by chance cannot be a necessary being. For what exists by chance can be lost by chance and, as such, is not necessary. Because there is no reason for the factually necessary being to be, He could disappear for no reason, for there is some possible world in which He does not exist. And even an omnipotent and factually necessary being could not keept Himself in existence, for that would be tantamount to causing Himself to be, which we have seen is impossible. It follows then that He is not indestructible. Hence the concept of a factually necessary being appears to be incoherent.

Furthermore, it is incompatible with other things the classical theist believes. For instance, it is one of the tenets of classical theism that God is the maximally greatest being. But a factually necessary being is not the maximally greatest being, for a being that exists in all worlds, the logically necessary being, is greater. For a being who is ontologically independent is greater than one whose existence is dependent upon chance. For these reasons and others it seems to us that the concept of a logically necessary being is superior to that of a factually necessary one, and more in harmony with classical theistic thought.

If God is the *the* being of which no greater can be conceived, then there can never be other gods with which He must compete. This is consistent with the Biblical tradition which teaches that although humans may worship some beings *as if* these beings were really gods (I Corinthians 8:4-6), there is only one true and living God by nature (Isaiah 43:10; 44:6,8; Galatians 4:8).

The reason that we have spent so much time discussing this aspect of classical theism is that necessity will play a large part in our critique of the Mormon concept of God. However, it should be noted here that we are not arguing for the *existence* of a necessary being, but rather we are examining the logical implications which follow if one does exist (In chapter 4 we will discuss some of the objections to the belief that there could exist a logically necessary being). Although we believe that it is perfectly rational to believe in the existence of a necessary being,[51] the existence or non-existence of such a being is not germane to this discussion. What is germane to this discussion is whether there are philosophical problems with the Mormon *concept* of God which make it incoherent (see chapters 3 and 4), and whether the classical *concept* of God makes sense (which we believe we have adequately presented and defended in this chapter) and is consistent with the portrayal of God found in the Bible (see chapter 5).

NOTES FOR CHAPTER ONE

1. Plato, *Timeaus*.

2. Baha'i writer J.E. Esslemont writes, "Baha'u'llah [the founder of Baha'ism] teaches that the universe is without beginning in time. It is a perpetual emanation from the Great First Cause." (J.E. Esslemont, *Baha'u'llah and the New Era*, 3rd ed. [Wilmette, IL: Baha'i Publishing Trust, 1970), p. 204. For critiques of Baha'ism, see Francis J. Beckwith, *Baha'i* (Minneapolis: Bethany House, 1985), and Francis J. Beckwith, "Baha'i-Christian Dialogue: Some Key Issues Considered," *Christian Research Journal* 11 (Winter/Spring, 1989): 15-19.

3. Blake Ostler, "The Mormon Concept of God," *Dialogue: A Journal of Mormon Thought* 17 (Summer 1984): 90.

4. We believe that this has been accomplished. See Francis J. Beckwith, *David Hume's Argument Against Miracles: A Critical Analysis* (Lanham, MD: University Press of America, 1989), chapter 5; and Francis J. Beckwith, "Are Creationists Philosophically and Scientifically Justified in Postulating God?: A Critical Analysis of Naturalistic Evolution," *Interchange* (Australia) 46 (1989): 52-61.

5. Richard Swinburne, *The Coherence of Theism* (Oxford: Clarendon, 1977), p. 149.

6. Thomas Aquinas, *Summa Theologica*, I, 25, 3, as contained in *Introduction to Saint Thomas Aquinas*, ed. Anton C. Pegis (New York: The Modern Library, 1948), p. 231.

7. William L. Rowe, *Philosophy of Religion* (Encino, CA: Dickenson, 1978), p. 9.

8. Ronald H. Nash, *The Concept of God* (Grand Rapids, MI: Zondervan, 1983), p. 51. There are some theists who deny this view of omniscience and claim that God does not know the future. However, they do not deny that God knows everything. They argue that since the future is not a thing, because it has not happened yet, it is impossible that God know it. Hence, they conclude that God knows everything and yet does not know the future. For defenses of this position, see Clark Pinnock, "God Limits His Knowledge," in *Predestination and Free Will*, eds. David Basinger and Randall Basinger (Downers Grove, IL: InterVarsity Press, 1986), pp. 141-162; Richard Rice, "Divine Foreknowledge and Free-Will Theism," in *The Grace of God, The Will of Man*, ed. Clark H. Pinnock (Grand Rapids, MI: Academie/Zondervan, 1989), pp. 121-139; Richard Rice, *God's Foreknowledge and Man's Free Will* (Minneapolis: Bethany House, 1985); and Swinburne, *Coherence*, pp. 167-178. For responses to this view, see the responses to Pinnock by John Feinberg, Norman Geisler, and Bruce Reichenbach in *Predestination and Free Will*, pp. 163-177; William Lane Craig, *The Only Wise God* (Grand Rapids, MI: Baker Book House, 1987), pp. 39-44; Alan W. Gomes, "God in Man's Image: Foreknowledge, Freedom, and the 'Openness' of God," *Christian Research Journal* 10 (Summer 1987): 18-24; and Robert A. Morey, *Battle of the Gods* (Southbridge, MA: Crown Publications, 1989).

9. See Ostler, "The Mormon Concept of God," pp. 67-74; Kent Robson, "Omnipotence, Omnipresence, and Omniscience in Mormon Theology," in *Line Upon Line: Essays on Mormon Doctrine*, ed. Gary James Bergera (Salt Lake City, UT: Signature Books, 1989), pp. 67-76; and Kent Robson, "Time and Omniscience in Mormon Theology," *Sunstone* 5 (May/June 1980): 17-23.

10. A number of Christian scholars deny this definition of freedom and defend what is known as *compatibilism*, the view that free-will and determinism are compatible. For a defense of this view see John Feinberg, "God Ordains All Things," in *Predestination and Free Will*, pp. 17-43. See also the responses to this view by Geisler, Reichenbach and Pinnock in *Predestination and Free Will*, pp. 45-60.

11. Ostler, "The Mormon Concept of God," p. 71.

12. Craig, *The Only Wise God*, p. 74.

13. Swinburne, *Coherence*, p. 104.

14. W. Norris Clarke, *The Philosophical Approach to God* (Winston-Salem, NC: Wake Forest University Publications, 1979), p. 108.

15. W. Norris Clarke, "A New Look at the Immutability of God," in *God, Knowable and Unknowable*, ed. Robert J. Roth (New York: Fordham University Press, 1973), p. 48.

16. Ostler, "The Mormon Concept of God," p. 74.

17. *Ibid.*, p. 76.

18. Geisler in *Predestination and Free Will*, p. 17. Some of our clarifications of the classical attributes serve the theist well in responding to some of the other objections to classical theism (which are often employed by Mormon theologians and philosophers) which fall outside the narrow scope of our discussion, such as the problem of evil and the exclusivity of salvation through Christ. Examples of such an application include, William Lane Craig, "'No Other Name': A Middle Knowledge Perspective on the Exclusivity of Salvation Through Christ," *Faith and Philosophy* 6 (April 1989): 172-188; and Alvin Plantinga, *God, Freedom, and Evil* (Grand Rapids, MI: Eerdmans, 1974)

19. Ostler, "The Mormon Concept of God," p. 76. The Mormon Scriptures teach that "spirit" is not immaterial, but a more fine and pure form of matter (*Doctrine & Covenants*, 131:7-8).

20. See C. Glenn Kenadjian, "Is the Doctrine that God is Spirit an Incoherent Concept?" *Journal of the Evangelical Theological Society* 31 (June 1988): 191-202; Richard Purtill, *Thinking About Religion: A Philosophical Introduction to Religion* (Englewood Cliffs, NJ: Prentice-Hall, 1978), pp. 123-152; and Swinburne, *Coherence*, pp. 106-125.

21. J.P. Moreland, *Scaling the Secular City* (Grand Rapids, MI: Baker Book House, 1987), p. 80.

22. See *Ibid.*, pp. 77-103.

23. *Ibid.*, p. 92.

24. *Ibid.*, p. 96.

25. See J.P. Moreland, "The Emergent Property View of the Self and the Bundle Theory: A Development Without Substance," *Bulletin of the Evangelical Philosophical Society* 11 (1988): 66-81; Moreland, *Scaling*, pp. 96-103; and Richard Swinburne, *The Evolution of the Soul* (Oxford: Clarendon, 1986).

26. This is a version of the kalam cosmological argument. For defenses of this argument, see Beckwith, *David Hume*, pp. 73-84; Beckwith, "Are Creationists Philosophically and Scientifically Justified in Postulating God?"; William Lane Craig, *The Kalam Cosmological Argument* (New York: Barnes & Noble, 1979); and Moreland, *Scaling*, pp. 18-42.

27. For example, see Beckwith, *David Hume*, pp. 75-76; Beckwith, "Are Creationists Philosophically and Scientifically Justified in Postulating God?," pp. 55-56; William Lane Craig, *The Existence of God and the Beginning of the Unverse* (San Bernardino, CA: Here's Life, 1979), p. 83; David Hume, *Letters of David Hume*, 2 vols., ed. J.Y.T. Greig (Oxford: Clarendon, 1932), 1:187; Moreland, *Scaling*, pp. 38-41; and Richard Taylor, *Metaphysics*, 2nd ed. (Englewood Cliffs, NJ: Prentice-Hall, 1974), p. 104.

28. See Robert Jastrow, *God and the Astronomers* (New York: Norton, 1978); and Anthony Kenny, *The Five Ways: St. Thomas Aquinas' Proofs for God's Existence* (New York: Schocken Books, 1969), p. 66.
   According to four of the world's most prominent astronomers, the big bang theory points towards a beginning of the universe at which time and space had their origin: "The universe began from a state of infinite density. Space and time were created in that event and so was all the matter in the universe. It is not meaningful to ask what happened before the big bang; it is somewhat like asking what is north of the north pole. Similarly, it is not sensible to ask where the big bang took place. The point-universe was not an object isolated in space; it was the entire universe, and so the only answer can be that the big bang happened everywhere." (J. Richard Gott III, James E. Gunn, David N. Schramm, Beatrice M. Tinsley, "Will the Universe Expand Forever?" *Scientific American* [March 1976]: 65)

29. See Beckwith, *David Hume*, pp. 76-82; Craig, *The Existence of God*, pp. 37-53; Moreland, *Scaling*, pp. 22-33; and Purtill, *Thinking*, pp. 52-55.

30. See J.L. Mackie, *The Miracle of Theism* (Oxford: Clarendon, 1982), pp. 92-95; and Richard Sorabji, *Time, Creation, and the Continuum* (Ithaca, NY: Cornell University Press, 1983), pp. 210-224.

31. *Ibid*.

32. Craig, *The Existence of God*, p. 87.

33. Moreland, *Scaling*, p. 42.

34. For a brief overview of the debate, see Nash, *Concept of God*, pp. 73-83. Classical theists who defend the position that God exists in time include Swinburne (*Coherence*, pp. 215-222), Nicholas Wolterstorff ("God Everlasting," in *God and the Good*, eds. Clifton Orlebeke and Lewis Smedes [Grand Rapids, MI: Eerdmans, 1975], pp. 181-203), and Craig (*The Existence of God*, pp. 86-89), although Craig believes that God was timeless prior to creation and created time along with all existence, but placed Himself within time at the moment of creation so that He can adequately interact with His creatures.

35. Plato, *Euthyphro*, 10a. Taken from *The Collected Dialogues of Plato*, eds. Edith Hamilton and Huntington Cairns (Princeton, NJ: Princeton University Press, 1961.

36. Bertrand Russell, *Why I Am Not A Christian* (New York: Simon & Schuster, 1957), p. 590.

37. Norman L. Geisler and Winfried Corduan, *Philosophy of Religion*, 2nd ed. (Grand Rapids, MI: Baker Book House, 1988), pp. 114-115.

38. *Ibid.*, p. 115. Geisler and Corduan also provide as an answer one put forth by those theists who follow in the tradition of William of Ockham. These theists admit "that the moral law flows from the will of God but deny that this is arbitrary and wrong. If God's will is the ultimate, then what God wills is the ultimate basis for all right and wrong." (*Ibid.*) However, Geisler and Corduan believe that of the two alternatives the Thomistic answer is more plausible, although "either one would invalidate Russell's disproof." (*Ibid.*)

39. For a philosophical defense of the miraculous, see Beckwith, *David Hume*.

40. Some theists, such as Norman Geisler (*Signs and Wonders* [Wheaton, IL: Tyndale House, 1988]), believe that this gift (along with the other "sign gifts") ceased functioning with the departure of Christ's apostles. Other theists, such C. Peter Wagner (*The Third Wave of the Holy Spirit* [Ann Arbor, MI: Servant, 1988]), do not agree. See Francis J. Beckwith's review of both these books in *Journal of the Evangelical Theological Society* 33 (September 1990): 394-398.

41. For a philosophical appraisal of petitionary prayer, see the articles by Terence Penelhum ("Petitionary Prayer") and Eleonore Stump ("Petionary Prayer") in *Miracles*, ed. Richard Swinburne (New York: Macmillan, 1989), pp. 153-166, 167-188.

42. For a brief discussion of this debate, see Nash, *Concept of God*, pp. 107-112.

43. Swinburne, *Coherence*, pp. 233-253.

44. St. Anselm, *Proslogium* in *Basic Writings*, 2nd ed., trans. S.N. Deane (LaSalle, IL: Open Court, 1962), p. 53.

45. Plantinga, *God, Freedom, and Evil*, p. 108.

46. *Ibid.*, p. 111. In order to avoid any confusion, we left out the numbers that Plantinga placed in front of these two propositions.

47. William Lane Craig, *The Cosmological Argument from Plato to Leibniz* (London: Harper & Row, 1980), p. 288.

48. Samuel Clarke, *A Discourse Concerning the Being and Attributes of God*, as quoted in William L. Rowe, *The Cosmological Argument* (Princeton, NJ: Princeton University Press, 1975), p. 182.

49. Rowe, *The Cosmological Argument*, p. 202.

50. Nash, *Concept of God*, p. 112.

51. Beckwith defends the rationality of belief in God in chapter 5 of his *David Hume* and in his article, "Are Creationists Philosophically and Scientifically Justified in Postulating God?". Stephen E. Parrish defends the rationality of theism in his Wayne State University doctoral dissertation (1991), "Necessary Being and the Theistic Arguments."

2
MORMON FINITISTIC THEISM

In oppostion to the infinite God of classical theism, there has been a rival tradition of finite theism, which has an impressive list of names supporting it. Edgar Sheffield Brightman (1884-1953), himself a believer in a finite God, lists Plato (428-347 B.C.), Epicurus (342?-?270 B.C.), Pierre Bayle (1647-1706), John Stuart Mill (1806-1873), F.C.S. Schiller (1864-1937), William James (1842-1910), Henri Bergson (1859-1941), A.N. Whitehead (1861-1947), and Peter A. Bertocci (1910-1989), along with many other adherents.[1] Hence, Mormon theism does not stand alone in the history of Western philosophical theology.

The concept of a finite God varies from thinker to thinker, but it is possible to identify some common traits. God, according to many finitistic theists, like Mill and Brightman, is a personal being like the God of classical theism. He is also all-good and all-benevolent. But there are large differences between the finite God and the classical God in other attributes.

God for Mill, Brightman and other finitistic theists is limited in power and in knowledge. He is not the creator of all that is, but rather exists alongside some other reality over which he has limited control. In addition, the God of finitistic theism is mutable, he is subject to change, as opposed to the God of classical theism, who is changeless (in the above way in which we defined "changeless").

There is one attribute that the other finitistic theists like Mill and Brightman give to God that is not shared by the Mormons. For Mill and Brightman, God is spirit and not a material being. As we shall see, Mormon theology teaches that God is in some sense corporeal.

For most of the finitistic theists, God is not a necessary being, at least not in the sense that we have attributed to the God of classilogical necessity of God. The God concept that Hartshorne proposes is both contingent in some respects, and necessary in others (as he puts it, finite at one pole and infinite at the other). We shall say more about Hartshorne later in chapter 4 of this book.

This brings us to a distinction among finitistic philosophers. Some finitists say that God is limited in some attributes, but not in others. Thus, Brightman says:

> God's will, then is in a definite sense finite. But we have called him "finite-infinite." Although the power of his will is limited by The Given [i.e., the non-rational limiting forces in the divine nature which are neither created nor sanctioned by God's will], arguments for the objectivity of ideals give ground for the postulate that his will for goodness and love is unlimited; likewise he is infinite in time and space, by his unbegun and unending duration and by his inclusion of all nature within his experience; such a God must also be unlimited in his knowledge of all that is, although human freedom and the nature of The Given probably limit his knowledge of the precise details of the future.[2]

Other finitists, such as the Mormons and Mill, tend to define God's finitude more narrowly. Writes Mill:

> A Being of great but limited power, how or by what limited we cannot even conjecture; of great, and perhaps unlimited intelligence, but perhaps, also, more narrowly limited than his power: who desires, and pays some regard to, the happiness of his creatures, but who seems to have other motives of action which he cares more for, and who can hardly be supposed to have created the universe for that purpose alone. Such is the Deity who Natural Religion points to; and any idea of God more captivating than this comes only from human wishes, or from the teaching of either real or imaginary Revelation.[3]

Thus Mill seems to support a God finite in all attributes, although at times he seems to allow for the possibility of some of God's attributes being infinite. On the whole, however, finitists emphasize the finite aspects of God.

Mormon theism lies at the opposite end of the theistic spectrum from classical theism. For the Mormons, God is like a man evolved to the highest extent. The finitistic philosophers, like Mill, James, and Brightman, moved the conception of God closer to the nature of man. But before any of them, the Mormons developed a concept of God which took the idea of finitistic theism to what is perhaps its logical conclusion.

As we noted in the introduction, since Mormonism is a religion, and a supposed revealed religion at that, there are more difficulties in presenting an accurate synopsis of its doctrines than those of a philosopher. Mormonism's doctrine of God is spread around several works regarded as scripture, and in the sayings and writings of its theologians, especially the presidents of the church who are thought to be divinely inspired. Fortunate ly, besides these sources there are also the works of several Mormon philosophers who have recently tried to put Mormon doctrine into a more coherent philosophical system.[4] Among those Mormon philosophers who present an apologetic for Mormon theism, probably the most important is David Lamont Paulsen, a Professor of Philosophy at Brigham Young University, whose doctoral dissertation in philosophy was entitled *The Comparative Coherency of Mormon (Finitistic) and Classical Theism*. It is by far the most detailed and comprehensive defense of Mormon theism with which we are familiar. Paulsen details the sources from which he draws his doctrine:

> In articulating the unique features of LDS [Mormon] theology, I shall rely on (1) doctrinal statements found in the primary LDS datum discourse which includes the *Pearl of Great Price*, the *Book of Mormon*, the *Doctrine and Covenants*, and the *Holy Bible*. These books have been officially sanctioned as scripture and as doctrinal canon for the church; (2) doctrinal statements of Joseph Smith which, although lacking doctrinal canonization, are almost universally accepted as normative for LDS theology; (3) doctrinal statements of presidents of the church, who as successors of Joseph Smith, are uniquely entitled to speak authoritatively on points of doctrine; (4) propositions entailed by or inferable from the aforesaid doctrinal statments; and (5) principles which are consistent with (as contrasted with entailed by) the datum discourse.[5]

Because of so many divergent sources of doctrine, there is a problem in affirming precisely what the Mormons believe. For example, because the *Book of Mormon* (1830, first edition) seems to teach a strongly Judaic monotheism with modalistic overtones (see Alma 11:26-31,38,38; Moroni 8:18; Mosiah 3:5-8; 7:27; 15:1-5) and the *Pearl of Great Price* (1851, first edition) clearly teaches polytheism (see Abraham, 4-5), a number of scholars have argued that Mormon theology evolved from a traditional monotheism to a uniquely American polytheism.[6] For these reasons, our chief concern will be the concept of God which we believe is currently held by the Mormon church, whose leaders believe they have accurately derived from the five sources of doctrine Paulsen has summarized. Despite the fact that there is disagreement among Mormon scholars about some precise points of doctrine, we believe that one can assert that the basic beliefs about God currently taught by the Mormon church include, but are not limited to, the claim that God is (1) personal and embodied, (2) organizer of this world, but subject to the laws and principles of a beginningless universe, (3) limited in power, (4) limited in knowledge, (5) not omnipresent in being, (6) mutable, (7) subject to values and eternal principles external to God, (8) able to communicate with humans, and (9) contingent and one of many gods.

And although there are undoubtedly individual Mormons who may hold to views of God which conflict with one or more of the above nine points, they no doubt would be out of step with the latter writings of Joseph Smith (which we presume take precedence over his earlier, and more classically orthodox writings), which clearly assert the above points.

Now let us clarify these points by contrasting the Mormon concept of God with the classical concept of God we presented in chapter 1 (see chart 2.1).

Chart 2.1

Classical Concept of God	Mormon Concept of God
1. Personal and disembodied	Personal and embodied.
2. Creator and Sustainer of all contingent existence.	Organizer of this world, but subject to the laws and principles of a beginningless universe
3. Omnipotent	Limited in power
4. Omniscient	Limited in knowledge
5. Omnipresent in being	Not omnipresent in being
6. Immutable	Mutable
7. The source of all values and perfectly good.	Subject to values and principles external to God.
8. Able to communicate with humans	Able to communicate with humans
9. Necessary and the only God	Contingent and one of many gods who exist

---

PERSONAL AND EMBODIED

First, for both classical and Mormon theism, God is personal. However, the Mormons believe that God has a body of flesh and bones, and hence deny that he is disembodied. As Joseph Smith writes: "The Father has a body of flesh and bones as tangible as man's; the Son's also..."[7]

ORGANIZER OF THE WORLD, BUT SUBJECT TO THE LAWS AND PRINCIPLES OF A BEGINNINGLESS UNIVERSE

As for the second attribute listed, creator and sustainer of existence, classical and Mormon theism are greatly at odds. Smith had this to say:

> You asked the learned doctors why they say the world was made out of nothing, and they will answer, "Doesn't the Bible say he *created* the world?" And they infer, from the word create, that it must have been made out of nothing. Now, the word create came from the word *baurau*, which does not mean to create out of nothing; it means... to organize the world out of chaos—chaotic matter, which is element, and in which dwells all the glory. Element had an existence from the time he had. The pure principles of element which can never be destroyed; they may be organized and reorganized, but not destroyed. They had no beginning, and can have no end.[8]

The notion of an uncreated and indestructible universe is reiterated by the noted Mormon theologian John A. Widtsoe:

> The Gospel holds strictly to the conception of a material universe. Much inconsistency of thought has come from the notion that things may be derived from an immaterial state, that is, from nothingness. This unthinkable view has been made the basis of doctrines concerning God and man, which have led to utter confusion of thought. The Gospel accepts the view, supported by all human experience, that matter occurs in many forms, some visible to the eye, other invisible, and yet others that may not be recognized by any of the senses of man. Spiritual matter is but a refined form of gross matter. In short, there is no such thing as immaterial matter, but some forms are more refined than others.[9]

Later on in the same work, Widtsoe goes on to say:

> God, possessing the supreme intelligence of the universe, can cause energy in accomplishing his ends, but create it, or destroy it, he cannot. Undiminished, everacting universal energy will continue

through all time. The sum of matter and energy, whether they are different or alike, will always remain the same.[10]

Here Mormon and classical theism stand in starkest contradiction. Not only do Mormons deny the doctrine of creation out of nothing, but they also deny that God has anything to do with sustaining the universe. As far as the existence of matter and energy goes, it is totally beyond God's control.

LIMITED IN POWER

The next property that is usually attributed to the God of classical theism is that of omnipotence. God is supposed to be able to do anything consistent with his perfect attributes, except that which is logically impossible or contradictory. The Mormon God is quite a bit different, insofar as being very limited in what he is able to do. The above selections which we have quoted show that there are at least some things that the Mormons believe that their God cannot do. For example, He cannot destroy or create matter and its laws. He is also subject to other limitations. To quote Brigham H. Roberts, who was perhaps the Mormons' greatest thinker on this point:

> ...[N]ot even God may place himself beyond the boundary of space: nor on the outside of duration. Nor is it conceivable to human thought that he can create space, annihilate matter. These are things that limit even God's omnipotence. What then, is meant by the ascription of the attribute of Omnipotence to God? Simply that all that may or can be done by power conditioned by other eternal—existences duration, space, matter, truth, justice—God can do. But even he may not act out of harmony with the other eternal existences which condition or limit even him.[11]

Thus for Mormons, omnipotence does not mean the same thing that it does for the classical theist. Furthermore, this view of omnipotence has a direct bearing upon the Mormon conception of the miraculous. To quote James E. Talmage, a Mormon Apostle and leading theologian:

> Miracles are commonly regarded as occurrences in opposition to the laws of nature. Such a conception is plainly erroneous, for the laws of nature are inviolable. However, as human understanding of these laws is at best but imperfect, events strictly in accordance with these laws may appear contrary thereto. The entire constitution of nature is ground on system and order; the laws of nature, however, are graded as are the laws of man. This operation of higher law in any

particular case does not destroy the causality of an inferior one.... All miracles are accomplished *through* the operation of the laws of nature.[12]

That is to say, since God is not the creator or sustainer of natural law, He does not have the *power* to suspend, alter, or change natural law, but He does have the power to *use* natural law to perform what we humans *perceive* to be a miracle. This is why Mormon philosopher Sterling McMurrin writes that "the traditional notion of miracle as suspension of natural law is usually denied by Mormon writers in favor of the interpretation that an event is miraculous only in the sense that the causal laws describing it are unknown to us.... From the divine perspective there are no miracles."[13]

LIMITED IN KNOWLEDGE

When it comes to the doctrine of omniscience, Mormons appear to be divided. Some Mormons seem to believe a view of omniscience which is consistent with classical theism,[14] that God has perfect knowledge of the past, present and future. On the other hand, there is a much more dominant tradition in Mormonism which teaches that God knows everything that can possibly be known, but only that which is actually occurring (the present) or has occurred (the past) can possibly be known. And since the future is not actual and hence cannot possibly be known, God does not know the future. Therefore, God is omniscient because He knows everything that can possibly be known, yet He increases in knowledge as the future unfolds and becomes the present.[15] Since this latter view of omniscience separates Mormonism from classical theism, we will be concerned only with this view and not with the Mormon view which is consistent with classical theism. Defending the dominant Mormon view, Roberts writes that this view is saying

> ...not that God is Omniscient up to the point that further progress in knowledge is impossible to him; but that all knowledge that is, all that exists, God knows.... He knows all that is known.[16]

In a similar vein, Paulsen comments, "This definition of God's omniscience allows for the possibility that some propositions may not be presently known or knowable (e.g., some asserting the future categorically free acts of persons)."[17] A number of Mormon philosophers, such as Blake Ostler and Kent Robson,[18] defend this view because they believe that it avoids one of the traditional problems with the classical concept of God, namely, the apparent inconsistency in affirming at the same time both God's omniscience and human free will (to which we believe we have responded in chapter 1). Ostler writes: "Given human free-agency, it is impossible to know the future because the future is yet undecided; therefore, propositions about the future are neither true nor false, but yet to be determined."[19] Hence, for Mormon theism, God knows everything that it is logically possible for any being to know. And since it is logically impossible for any being to know the future, the future is open and God does not know what will inevitably happen. Mormon philosophers and theologians believe that this view best preserves human free-will.

Ostler points out that this view of omniscience, in comparison with the classical view of omniscience, seems more consistent with other important aspects of the Mormon concept of God:

> Creation is viewed in both Mormonism and process philosophy as an ongoing act of bringing order out of chaos and enhancing personal potential through increasing intergration.... Rejection of absolute omniscience is consistent with Mormonism's committment to the inherent freedom of uncreated selves, the temporal progression of deity, the moral responsibility of humans, and the consequential denial of salvation by arbitrary grace alone.[20]

NOT OMNIPRESENT IN BEING

Unlike the God of classical theism who is omnipresent in being, the God of Mormon theism is only omnipresent insofar as he is aware of everything in the universe simultaneously. Since God has a physical body, and hence is limited by time and space, God's being cannot be present everywhere. Roberts writes that the omnipresence of God

> must be so far limited as to be ascribed to God's Spirit, or Influence, or Power: but not of God as a Person or Individual; for in these latter respects even God is limited by the law that one body cannot occupy two places at one and the same time. But radiating from his presence, as beams of light and warmth radiate from the sun, is God's spirit, penetrating and permeating space, making space and all worlds in space vibrate with his life and thought and presence: holding all forces—dynamic and static—under control, making them to subserve his will and purposes.
> God also uses other agencies to reflect himself, his power or authority; also his Wisdom, Goodness, Justice and Mercy—angels and arch-angels both in heaven and on earth; and in the earth prophets, apostles, teachers—all that make for up-lift, for righteousness; all

that catch some ray of the Divine Spirit in poem, music, painting sculpture, statecraft, or mechanical arts—all these but reflect God and are a means of multiplying and expressing him, the Divine. And in a special way, as witness for God, and under very special conditions, the Holy Ghost, that Being accounted the Third Person of the Godhead —he reflects and stands for God, his Power, and Wisdom; his Justice, Truth, and Mercy—for all that can be, or is, called God, or is God. All these means, direct and indirect, convey God into the universe, and keep himself everywhere present in all his essentials of Wisdom, Power, and Goodness, while his bodily presence remains at the center of it all.[21]

Hence, when a Mormon says that God is omnipresent he is asserting that God's influence, power, and knowledge is all-pervasive, but that the focal point of God's being (that is, his body) exists at a particular place in time and space. Because the Mormons do not believe that the universe is contingent upon God to sustain its continued existence, there is no need for the Mormons to defend the classical view of omnipresence.

MUTABLE

Classical theism teaches that God never changes in His essential nature. God has always been God. There never was a time when God did not possess all His infinite attributes. God does not become stronger, more knowledgable, or more perfect. He is already essentially perfect in every attribute. Mormonism, on the other hand, teaches that God is a being who has not always been God. God was once a man on another planet who, by the laws of eternal progression and through obedience to the precepts of his God, eventually attained Godhood himself. As a God he in turn "created" this world out of both pre-existent inorganic matter and pre-existent intelligences (what an individual human self is prior to being "organized") from which human spirits are organized. Mormon scholar Hyrum L. Andrus writes:

> Though man's spirit is organized from a pure and fine substance which possesses certain properties of life, Joseph Smith seems to have taught that within each individual spirit there is a central primal intelligence (a central directing principle of life), and that man's central primal intelligence is a personal entity possessing some degree of life and certain rudimentary cognitive powers before the time the human spirit was organized.[22]

And once spirits are organized they begin their progressive journey from mortality to their inevitable fate, which will end in Godhood if they obey and follow the precepts of their God (on this planet, the precepts are found in the Mormon religion). Furthermore, given our account of the Mormon view of omniscience, God's knowledge is increasing, and hence God is changing in respect to his knowledge. Although some Mormon scholars, such as Bruce McConkie,[23] have taught that once God attained the fullness of Godhood he changes only insofar as having "his kingdoms increase and his dominions multiply, not in the sense that he learns new truths and discovers new laws,"[24] others, such as B.H. Roberts, Brigham Young, and Wilford Woodruff,[25] have taught that God "is increasing and progressing in knowledge, power, and dominion and will do so worlds without end."[26] No matter which way the Mormons think of God's mutability, the upshot is that the God of Mormonism is radically mutable in comparison to the God of traditional theism.

SUBJECT TO VALUES AND ETERNAL PRINCIPLES EXTERNAL TO GOD

It is apparent from what we have covered thus far that the Mormon God is subject to certain eternal forces and principles. This is also true of moral values. And for this reason, unlike the God of classical theism, the Mormon God is not the source of all values and is not eternally perfect. To quote Paulsen:

> In accord with classical theism, Mormon theism affirms that God perfectly exemplifies every moral value. That is, He is perfectly just, loving, kind, compassionate, veracious, no respecter of persons, etc. But his perfections are not eternal, but were acquired by means of developmental process.
> God, then, according to Mormon theology, is not unconditioned or unlimited. He is limited at least by other co-eternal existences: primal elements (mass-energy), space, time, primal intelligences (selves), and primal laws and principles. Nor has he always been "God." At some distant point in an infinite past, He earned the right to be "God" through a process which men, as his children, are now repeating.[27]

Since God Himself came into being as God (although he existed in some state eternally), He cannot be the source and sanction of values. He Himself obeys laws and affirmed values for whose existence he is not responsible.

ABLE TO COMMUNICATE WITH HUMANS

Classical theists and Mormons agree that God is able to communicate with humans and that humans can communicate with God. However, Mormons and classical theists disagree as to which Scriptures are God's chief way of communicating to His people. For instance, many classical theists in the Christian tradition claim that the Bible is God's only way of communicating to His people. They believe that the Bible is the only infallible standard for faith and practice. But as we noted earlier, although accepting the authority of the Bible, Mormons also accept as authoritative revelation the *Book of Mormon, Doctrine and Covenants, Pearl of Great Price,* and the subsequent revelations of those who have occupied the Mormon presidency (those who have succeeded Joseph Smith as prophet of the church). And because Mormons interpret the Biblical text in the light of their own unique revelations, they find apparent agreement between their concept of God and the concept of God found in the Bible. But as we shall see in chapter 5, this agreement is very superficial, for Mormon apologists commit a number of exegetical and hermeneutical fallacies while interpreting the Bible.

CONTINGENT AND ONE OF MANY GODS

All of this brings us to a very important distinction between the God of the Mormons and the God of classical theism. The God of classical theism is one God. He is the only source of everything else that exists. Being *the* greatest conceivable being, there neither are nor can be other Gods with which He must compete. With this the philosophers of the finitistic theistic position (Brightman, Mill, etc.) have not disagreed. Their God is not the greatest conceivable being, but He is the only God. Thus, both classical theists and the finitistic theists are monotheists. Not so the Mormons. In the most radical break with classical theism, the Mormons return to polytheism.[28] In the thought of the finitistic philosophers, God has to struggle with some other reality that exists apart from him; for Mill the material universe, for Brightman it is the "Given" (that part of God's own nature that is outside of His control). In Mormon thought God must, as we have seen, contend not only with the material universe and the laws that govern it, but also with uncreated selves. As we said when we were discussing the Mormon God's mutability, each individual is eternal, along with God, but in different degrees of development. Truman Madsen, a Mormon philosopher, writes:

> The quantity, though not the quality, of selves is fixed forever. It is infinite. There is no beginning to our "beginning." Mind has no birthday and memory has no first (birthday). Age is relative only in stages, not existence. No one is older or younger than anyone else. We have always been alone, separate from, and always together, coexistent with, other intelligences. Creation is never totally original; it is always a combination of prior realities. Immortality is in no sense conditional. It is inevitable and universal, even for subhuman intelligences.... Through all transformations of eternity, no self can change completely into another thing. Identity remains.[29]

By organizing this world out of pre-existent matter, the Mormon God gives these organized spirits the opportunity to possess bodies and eventually attain godhood like himself if they follow the precepts of Mormonism. Hence, the God of Mormonism was organized by his God who himself is a "creature" of another God and so on and so on *ad infinitum*.[30] Since these selves have the possibility of becoming gods, the question may arise: What is the number of gods that currently exist? Orson Pratt, a Mormon theologian, wrote, "If we take a million worlds like this and number their particles, we should find there are more Gods than there are particles of matter in those worlds."[31] Parley P. Pratt implies that these gods exist in an infinite space, when he states that "there has always existed a boundless infinitude of space."[32] Hence, it follows from what we have covered thus far that in Mormon thought there is an infinite spatial expanse, an infinite temporal duration, an infinite amount of matter and an infinite number of primal intelligences. It seems to us that there are also an infinite number of gods implied by this scheme, although we have found no explicit statement by the Mormons that this is actually the case.

It should be obvious that the Mormon God is not logically necessary. There are many possible worlds in which He does not exist. Even according to Mormon theology, He might not have existed as a God in this world. The Mormons believe in freedom of the will. Their definition of freedom of the will is radically libertarian; things could have easily been different than they are.[33] It could have been the case that their God could have chosen or acted differently than He actually did, and thus failed to become a God. Therefore, the Mormon God is *contingent* in an infinite lineage of gods, and is not logically necessary.

In order to clarify what we mean when we say that the Mormon God is "contingent," we want to briefly address the claim that the Mormon God is not contingent because Mormonism teaches that the ultimate constituents of the universe are *necessary* beings, *not* contingent ones. For example, Blake Ostler writes:

In contrast to the self-sufficient and solitary absolute who creates *ex nihilo* (out of nothing), the Mormon God did not bring into being the ultimate constituents of the cosmos—neither its fundamental matter nor the space/time matrix which defines it. Hence, unlike the Necessary Being of classical theology who alone could not *not* exist and on which all else is contingent for existence, the personal God of Mormonism confronts uncreated realities which exist of metaphysical necessity. Such realities include inherently self-directing selves (intelligences), primordial elements (mass/energy), the natural laws which structure reality, and moral principles grounded in the intrinsic value of selves and the requirements for growth and happiness.[34]

It is apparent that Mormonism teaches a metaphysical pluralism in which certain basic realities exist necessarily, i.e., they are indestructible and have always existed. But this is not what traditional theists mean when they say that God exists necessarily. As we noted in the first chapter, they mean either that God is *factually* necessary, in the sense that He is the being on which everything else depends for its existence, or they widen this concept and assert that He is *logically* necessary, in the sense that He is the only being who exists in every possible world (and we feel that the latter is the best option for theism). In both cases, God is thought of as existing independently of everything else; that is, if everything dependent ceased to exist, God would still exist. But the fact is that in the Mormon scheme of things each "necessary" existent cannot exist on its own, but is metaphysically dependent on other "necessary" existents. For example, if the space/time matrix did not exist, none of the self-directing selves would exist. Furthermore, if God had not obeyed certain moral principles prior to attaining Godhood, he would have never become God. Hence, God could not exist unless certain other basic realities existed. And it is in this sense that we say that the Mormon God is contingent. Therefore, if one recognizes what Mormon scholars mean when they refer to God as "necessary" and what we mean by "contingent," there is no real dispute.

Sometimes Mormon scholars confuse the general public by presenting their unique theology in the confines of classical theistic terminology. For instance, as many Mormon thinkers, such as Ken Robson and O. Kendall White Jr.,[35] have pointed out, there is a movement among Mormon theologians and philosophers (White calls it "Mormon neo-orthodoxy") to apply to the Mormon God the "omnis" usually attributed to God by classical theists: omnipotence, omnipresence, omniscience, etc. As we have seen, these omnis do not apply to the Mormon God if one wants to maintain both their classical meanings and the traditional concept of the Mormon God, although this has not prevented some Mormons from using them. For example, the late Bruce McConkie writes that God is all-powerful and that this omnipotence "consists in having unlimited power...", and "[t]hose who obtain exaltation [i.e., Godhood] will gain more power and thus themselves be omnipotent."[36] But since Mormon theology also teaches that God is limited by time and space and the existence of other selves, McConkie must define omnipotence in a way that is inconsistent with the classical definition. He could say that a Mormon god possesses the *maximal power* any being can possibly possess while limited by other eternal self-existing entities. Although this would be consistent with Mormon theology, it would be quite different from the tradtional theistic conception which entails that God is the creator of time, space and all contingent reality, and is the only being that exists necessarily.

Hence, although some Mormon spokespersons employ traditional theological terminology, it is apparent that Mormons cannot really believe in the existence of a God with unlimited power in the traditional sense. This is why Mormon scholars like Robson and White believe that the incorporation of traditional terminology by the Mormon neo-orthodox will inevitably rob Mormon theology of both its uniqueness and its historic roots.

NOTES FOR CHAPTER TWO

1. Edgar Sheffield Brightman, *A Philosophy of Religion* (Englewood Cliffs, NJ: Prentice-Hall, 1940), pp. 295-300.

2. *Ibid.*, p. 337.

3. John Stuart Mill, *Nature, the Utility of Religion and Theism* (London: Longmans, Green and Co., 1923), pp. 194-195.

4. For example, Sterling McMurrin, *The Philosophical Foundations of Mormon Theology* (Salt Lake City: University of Utah Press, 1959); Sterling M. McMurrin, *The Theological Foundations of the Mormon Religion* (Salt Lake City: University of Utah Press, 1965); Blake Ostler, "The Mormon Concept of God," *Dialogue: A Journal of Mormon Thought* 17 (Summer 1984): 65-93; David Lamont Paulsen, *The Comparative Coherency of Mormon (Finitistic) and Classical Theism* (Ann Arbor, MI: University Microfilms, 1975); Kent Robson, "Omnis on the Horizon," *Sunstone* 8 (July-August 1983): 21-23; Kent Robson, "Time and Omniscience in Mormon Theology," *Sunstone* 5 (May-June 1980): 17-23; and O. Kendall White, Jr., *Mormon Neo-orthodoxy: A Crisis Theology* (Salt Lake City: Signature Books, 1987), pp. 57-67. White's work is more of a sociological rather than a philosophical work, although his presentation of the Mormon concept of God is extremely helpful.

5. Paulsen, *Comparative Coherency*, p. 66.

6. See James B. Allen, "Emergence of a Fundamental: The Expanding Role of Joseph Smith's First Vision in Mormon Religious Thought," *Journal of Mormon History* 7 (1980): 43-61; and Thomas G. Alexander, "The Reconstruction of Mormon Doctrine: From Joseph Smith to Progression Theology," *Sunstone* 5 (July/August 1980): 32-39.

7. *Doctrine & Covenants*, 130:22a. In the remaining part of the verse, Smith writes that "the Holy Ghost has not a body of flesh and bones, but is a personage of Spirit. Were it not so, the Holy Ghost could not dwell in us." Although the Holy Ghost is one of the three Gods that Mormons are chiefly concerned with religiously, our concern in this book is with the God the Mormons *currently* call the Father, Elohim, although this is *historically* problematic. For instance, see Boyd Kirkland, "Elohim and Jehovah in Mormonism and the Bible," *Dialogue: A Journal of Mormon Thought* 19 (Spring 1986): 77-93; and Boyd Kirkland, "Jehovah as the Father," *Sunstone* 9 (Autumn 1984): 36-44.

8. Joseph Smith, *History of the Church of Jesus Christ of Latter-day Saints*, 7 vols., intro. and notes B.H. Roberts (Salt Lake City: Deseret Books, 1978), 6: 308-309. (from now on, *HC*).

9. John A. Widtsoe, *A Rational Theology* (Salt Lake City: Deseret Books, 1915), p. 11.

10. *Ibid.*, p. 13.

11. B. H. Roberts, *Seventy's Course in Theology: Third Year and Fourth Year* (Salt Lake City, UT: The Caxton Press), 4: 70.

12. James E. Talmage, *The Articles of Faith* (Salt Lake City: Church of Jesus Christ of Latter-day Saints, 1957), pp. 220-223.

13. McMurrin, *Philosophical Foundations*, p. 19.

14. See Neal A. Maxwell, "A More Determined Discipleship," *Ensign* (February 1979), pp. 69-73; and Neal A. Maxwell, *All These Things Shall Give Thee Experience* (Salt Lake City: Deseret Books, 1979).
Maxwell writes, "The past, present, and future are before God *simultaneously....* Therefore, God's omniscience is not solely a function of prolonged and discerning familiarity with us—but of the stunning reality that the past, present, and future are part of an 'eternal now' with God." (Maxwell, *All These Things*, pp. 95-96). However, in defense of Maxwell (a member of the LDS Quorum of the Twelve Apostles), Blake Ostler writes, "In fairness to Elder Maxwell, we must recognize that his observations are meant as rhetorical expressions to inspire worship rather than as an exacting philosophical analysis of the idea of timelessness. Furthermore, in a private conversation in January 1984, Elder Maxwell told me that he is unfamiliar with the classical idea of timelessness and the problems it entails." (Ostler, "The Mormon Concept of God," p. 75).

15. Ostler cites four Mormon leaders who have held views consistent with this view of omniscience: Brigham Young, Wilford Woodruff, Lorenzo Snow, and B.H. Roberts. For references, see Ostler, "The Mormon Concept of God," pp. 76-78.

16. Roberts, *Seventy's*, 4: 70.

17. Paulsen, *Comparative Coherency*, p. 77.

18. Ostler, "The Mormon Concept of God," pp. 76-80; and Robson, "Time and Omniscience in Mormon Theology,"

19. Ostler, "The Mormon Concept of God," p. 78.

20. *Ibid.*, p. 79.

21. Roberts, *Seventy's* , 4: 70-71. See Bruce R. McConkie, *Mormon Doctrine*, 2nd ed. (Salt Lake City: Bookcraft, 1979), pp. 544-545.

22. Hyrum L. Andrus, *God, Man and the Universe* (Salt Lake City: Bookcraft, 1968), p. 175. The eternal pre-existence of human selves is taught by Joseph Smith in *HC*, 6: 310-313. For an excellent historical summary of the internal church controversy surrounding the correct interpretation of this doctrine, see Blake Ostler, "The Idea of Pre-existence in the Development of Mormon Thought," *Dialogue: A Journal of Mormon Thought* 15 (Spring 1982): 59-78.

23. Bruce McConkie, "The Seven Deadly Heresies," lecture delivered at Brigham Young University, June 1, 1980.

24. *Ibid.*

25. Roberts, *Seventy's*, 4: 69-70; Gary James Bergera, "The Orson Pratt-Brigham

Young Controversies: Conflict Within the Quorums, 1853-1868," *Dialogue: A Journal of Mormon Thought* 13 (Summer 1980); and Wilford Woodruff in *Journal of Discourses, by Brigham Young, President of the Church of Jesus Christ of Latter-day Saints, His Two Counsellors, the Twelve Apostles, and Others*, 26 vols., reported by G.D. Watt (Liverpool: F.D. Richards, 1854-1886), 6:120 (from now on *JD*).

26. Woodruff in *JD*, 6:120.

27. Paulsen, *Comparative Coherency*, p. 79.

28. Van Hale writes that although technically Mormonism is *polytheistic*, in the literal sense of believing in the existence of many gods, it is not *polytheistic* in the sense in which ancient Greek religion was polytheistic: there exist many rival gods, who engage in all sorts of immorality. For this reason, Hale writes that "a term acceptable to Mormons is *plurality of gods*. This phrase conveys the doctrine of many gods without polytheism's connotations of many sordid beings." (Van Hale, "Defining the Mormon Doctrine of Deity," *Sunstone* 10 [1985]: 25).
Although we will use the term "polytheism" in this work to describe the Mormon view of deity, it should be taken in the most literal sense of simply the belief that there exist many gods, and not in the sense of the belief in morally fallen deities, such as in Greek and Roman mythology.

29. Truman Madsen, *Eternal Man* (Salt Lake City: Deseret Books, 1966), p. 26.

30. Joseph Smith presents this idea when he states: "If Abraham reasoned thus—If Jesus Christ was the Son of God, and John discovered that God the Father of Jesus Christ had a Father, you may suppose that He had a Father also. Where was there ever a son without a father? And where was there ever a father without first being a son? Whenever did a tree or anything else spring into existence without a progenitor? And everything comes in this way." (*HC*, 6: 476).

31. *JD*, 2: 345.

32. Parley Pratt, *Key To Theology*, p. 43, as quoted in Andrus, *God, Man and the Universe*, p. 147.

33. For a brief overview of the Mormon view of free-will and freedom, see McMurrin, *Theological Foundations*, pp. 77-82.

34. Ostler, "The Mormon Concept of God," p. 67.

35. See Robson, "Omnis," and White, *Mormon Neo-Orthodoxy*.

36. McConkie, *Mormon Doctrine*, p. 544.

3
PHILOSOPHICAL PROBLEMS WITH THE MORMON CONCEPT OF GOD

Unlike their Christian counterparts,[1] Mormon theologians and philosophers spend very little time in critical examination of their own concept of God. Almost all of the articles and books on this topic, written by some of the most articulate and careful Mormon thinkers, usually consist of both a critical examination of what the authors believe is the classical concept of God and a demonstration of why the Mormon view is more religiously adequate.[2]

The purpose of this chapter is to present some philosophical difficulties we see with the Mormon concept of God, which are to our knowledge rarely if ever mentioned by Mormon scholars. We believe that the Mormon concept of God presents the Mormon theologian with at least four philosophical problems: (1) The impossibility of an infinite series of events in the past; (2) the impossibility of an eternal progression in a beginningless series of events; (3) the impossibility of an actual infinite number of things in the material world; and (4) the impossibility of achieving omniscience in time and space. In the next chapter we will discuss the philosophical problems with trying to show that the Mormon God exists by way of the design argument. This critique will give us another reason for thinking that the Mormon universe is fundamentally irrational. And in chapter 5 we will present a brief biblical critique of the Mormon concept of God.

THE IMPOSSIBILITY OF AN INFINITE SERIES OF EVENTS IN THE PAST

From its own view of God, it naturally follows that Mormonism holds that the past series of events in time is *beginningless*. Late Mormon president Joseph Fielding Smith writes that the "Prophet [i.e., Joseph Smith] taught that *our Father had a Father and so on*."[3] Heber C. Kimball, who was a member of the Mormon First Presidency, asserts that "we shall go back to our Father and God, who is connected with *one who is still farther back*; and this Father is connected with *one still further back, and so on*...."[4] Furthermore, McConkie writes that "the elements from which the creation took place are eternal and therefore had no beginning."[5] Mormon sociologist, O. Kendall White, writes that Mormon theology assumes metaphysical materialism and that this in turn "not only assumes that God and the elements exist necessarily, but so do space and time. In contrast, traditional Christian orthodoxy maintains that space and time, along with everything else except God, exist because God created them."[6] Therefore, Mormon metaphysics assumes that the past consists of an infinite series of events.

There is a philosophical problem in asserting that the series of events in the past is beginningless. Philosopher William Lane Craig has developed four arguments—two philosophical and two scientific—to show why there cannot be an infinite series of events in the past.[7] In this chapter we will look at Craig's second philosophical argument, which he presents in the following way:[8]

> 1. The series of events in time is a collection formed by adding one member after another.
> 2. A collection formed by adding one member after another cannot be actually infinite.
> 3. Therefore, the series of events in time cannot be actually infinite.

The first premise seems rather indisputable. For when one thinks of the series of events in time one does not think of them as happening simultaneously, but occurring one after another. For example, despite the tasteless jokes at bachelor parties, one's wedding and one's funeral do not happen at the same time: the first precedes the second (hopefully with a large number of years in between).

In the second premise we are arguing that "a collection formed by adding one member after another cannot be actually infinite." To help the reader come to grips with this premise, a brief review of what is meant by an infinite set in mathematics is in order. An infinite set of numbers is one that is complete and to which one cannot add, e.g., the infinite set of natural numbers: (1, 2, 3,... 10,... 1,000,001...). This set contains an *unlimited* number of digits from 1 to infinity. However, since an actual infinite is a *complete* set with an infinite amount of members, the series of events in time cannot be actually infinite (that is, beginningless). This is because the series of events in time is always increasing (being added to) and one can never arrive at infinity by adding one member after another. The following example should help to demonstrate this.

Suppose that you were driving on Interstate 15 from Las Vegas to Salt Lake City with 450 miles to cross; all things being equal, you would eventually arrive in Salt Lake. However, if you were to drive on an I-15 from Las Vegas to Salt Lake with an *infinite* number of miles to cross, you would never arrive in Salt Lake. But if you did arrive in Salt Lake, it would only prove that the distance was finite. Since an infinite number is unlimited, one can never complete an infinite number of miles.

Applying this to a beginningless universe, a certain absurdity develops: if the universe had no beginning, then every event has been preceded by an infinite number of events. But if one can never arrive at infinity by adding one member after another, one would have never arrived at the present day, because to do so one would have had to "cross" (or complete) an infinite number of days. In order to better understand this, philosopher J.P. Moreland provides another example:

> ...[S]uppose a person were to think backward through the events in the past. In reality, time and the events within it move in the other direction. But mentally he can reverse that movement and count backward farther and farther into the past. Now he will either come to a beginning or he will not. If he comes to a beginning, then the universe obviously had a beginning. But if he never could, even in principle, reach a first moment, then this means that it would be impossible to start with the present and run backward through all of the events in the history of the cosmos. Remember, if he did run through all of them, he would reach a first member of the series, and the finiteness of the past would be established. In order to avoid this conclusion, one must hold that, starting from the present, it is *impossible* to go backward through all of the events in history.
> But since events really move in the other direction, this is equivalent to admitting that if there was no beginning, the past could have never been exhaustively traversed to reach the present moment.[9]

Given the soundness of the above premises, it follows that the universe must have had beginning. But since Mormonism's concept of God hinges on the doctrine of eternal progression—that every God was once a man who eventually progressed to Godhood—and its metaphysic teaches that the elements are eternal, Mormon theology necessarily adheres to a universe with no beginning. I believe that the only way out of this dilemma is either to refute the above argument (which does not look too hopeful) or to amend the Mormon concept of God in such a way that Mormon theologians concede that the universe was created by a self-existent and necessary being at some finite time ago in the past. Consequently, if this being is Creator of everything, he would also be the creator of the God of Mormonism. But to concede this point Mormon theologians would be admitting that their basic metaphysic is untrue and that the God of the "gentiles" (Protestantism, Catholicism, and Eastern Orthodoxy) indeed exists and is a far greater being than their God.

Prior to moving on to the second philosophical problem with the Mormon concept of God, we want to make mention of several objections to the above argument. We will first look at two classical arguments, and then look at a couple of contemporary ones. Probably the most famous classical arguments come from Thomas Aquinas' defense of his admission that there is no clear philosophical proof for creation in time, since God could have created from all eternity.[10] Although Aquinas presents several arguments for this admission, I will focus on the two which have direct bearing upon the argument presented in this paper. First, he asserts that creation from all eternity does not involve a logical contradiction. Second, Aquinas argues that an infinite series of events in the past is possible. Concerning the first assertion, Aquinas writes:

> First of all, no cause that produces its effect instantaneously has to precede its effect in time. Now, God is a cause that produces his effect, not through movement, but instantaneously. Hence he does not have to precede his effect in time.... What is more, if there is ever a cause whose proceeding effect cannot co-exist at the same instant, the only reason would be the absence of some element needed for a complete causing; for a complete cause and its effect exist simultaneously. But God has never been incomplete. Therefore an effect caused by him can exist eternally, as long as he exists, and hence he need not precede it in time.... Hence, although God is recognized as an agent acting voluntarily, yet it follows that he can see to it that what he causes should never be non-existent.

And thus it is evident that no logical contradiction is implied in the statement that an agent does not precede its effect in time. God cannot, however, bring into being anything that implies logical contradiction.[11]

Several comments are in order. First, Aquinas' argument is certainly no option for the Mormon. For to avoid the reality of a finite past by saying that there exists a self-existent omnipotent being on which the universe is eternally contingent is to support classical theism, not Mormonism. Second, our argument against an infinite series of past events does not discount the possibility of an eternal creation; the two are not necessarily synonymous. James Sadowsky's comments on our argument are worth noting:

> It should be pointed out that this argument would not prove the non-eternity of the world to one who did believe in God. Such an individual could while granting the world has not been eternally in action still claim that until God moved it from inaction to action, it had existed from all eternity in a purely static condition.[12]

Therefore, since Mormon metaphysics demands the universe be eternally in action, the real obstacle is Aquinas' second argument. In defending the possibility of an infinite past, Aquinas argues in one place that one is attacking a straw man when one argues that because an infinite series cannot be traversed there cannot be an infinite series of events in the past. This is so because it "is founded on the idea that, given two extremes, there is an infinite number of mean terms." But the passage of time "is always understood as being from term to term." That is to say, "whatever by-gone day we choose, from it to the present day there is a finite number of days which can be traversed."[13] Bernardino Bonansea explains Aquinas' objection as saying that since there was no first moment in an eternal world, "no infinite distance is being traversed."[14]

Actually, the fact there was no first moment really is of no help, and is entirely irrelevant. In fact, the absence of a first term merely accentuates the problem of affirming an infinite past. For example, no doubt that when we discuss in 1991 the events of 1981, we make the judgment that the events of 1981 occurred 10 years ago and that a finite number of days have been traversed. The same goes for events that occurred 50, 100, or three million years ago. What Aquinas is arguing for is that no matter how far back one goes one will be traversing only a finite distance, and hence, one is not claiming to traverse an infinite. But this seems to vindicate our argument. For if one cannot in principle reach a day which occurred an infinite number of days ago—which is what Aquinas means when he asserts that "whatever by-gone day we choose, from it to the present day there is a finite number of days which can be traversed"—this only goes to prove the impossibility of traversing an actual infinite, which is the same thing as saying that all the events in the beginningless past could not have been crossed to reach today. Therefore, we do not see how Aquinas can effectively dispute our conclusion that a beginningless series of events in time is impossible.[15]

Among the contemporary philosophers who have disputed our argument are J.L. Mackie, William Wainwright, and Richard Sorabji. We will briefly cover what we believe are their strongest arguments. Both Mackie and Wainwright present an argument nearly identical to Aquinas' second argument.[16] Mackie writes that our argument "assumes that, even if past time were infinite, there would still have been a starting-point in time, but one infinitely remote, so that an actual infinity would have had to be traversed to reach the present from there." However, Mackie points out that "to take the hypothesis of infinity seriously would be to suppose that there was no starting-point, not even an infinitely remote one, and that from any specific point in past time there is only a finite stretch that needs to be traversed to reach the present."[17]

Like Aquinas' second argument, this one is also weak. First, as Moreland states, the defender of our argument "does *not* assume an infinitely distant beginning to the universe to generate his puzzles against traversing an actual infinite."[18] That is, the problems involved in traversing an actual infinite occur precisely because there is no beginning. As we pointed out in the critique of Aquinas' argument, if one cannot in principle reach a day which occurred an infinite number of days ago, this only goes to prove the impossibility of traversing an actual infinite. Second, it seems that Mackie and Wainwright are arguing that because each finite segment of an infinite series can be traversed in principle therefore a whole infinite series made up of finite segments can also be traversed. But this argument commits the informal fallacy of composition, which occurs when someone mistakenly argues that what is true of the part is also true of the whole. For example, just because each part of my car is light does not mean the entire car is light. Thus it is Mackie and Wainwright who do not take the infinite seriously.

Sorabji argues that our objection to an infinite past makes the mistake of confusing counting with traversing. He writes that it is impossible to count to infinity if one begins at a particular starting point. However, an infinite past has no starting point. Therefore, it is possible that an infinite past has been traversed.[19]

Several comments are in order. First, as Moreland points out, the criticisms against traversing an actual infinite are based on the *nature* of the actual infinite, *not* on the nature of counting. That is to say, whether one is talking about either starting a count from the number one or a beginningless series of events, it is an actual infinite number that is alleged will be or has been traversed.[20] Second, how does not having a starting point make an actual infinite suddenly traversable? Is it not true that an infinite series with a starting point and an infinite series with no beginning have the same amount of members? Why then is traversing the latter less difficult than traversing the former? Moreland present the following example:

> ... [A]ssume that someone had been counting toward zero from negative infinity from eternity past. If a person goes back in time from the present moment, he will *never* reach a point when he is finishing his count or engaging in the count itself. This is because at every point, he will have already had an infinity to conduct the count. As Zeno's paradox of the race course points out, the problem with such a situation is not merely that one cannot complete an infinite task; one cannot even start an infinite task from a beginningless situation. For one could never reach a determinate position in the infinite series which alone would allow the series to be traversed and ended at zero (the present moment).[21]

Hence, the absence of a beginning does not make traversing an actual infinite more likely, but actually accentuates the philosophical problems in believing that traversing an actual infinite is possible. As Craig has observed, such a task is like trying to jump out of a bottomless pit. Although there are other criticisms of our argument, they seem to be derived from the ones we have already covered. We refer the reader to the works which deal with these criticisms.[22] We believe, however, what has been covered are the strongest objections, which do not seem strong enough to overturn our argument.

THE IMPOSSIBILITY OF AN ETERNAL PROGRESSION IN A BEGINNINGLESS SERIES OF EVENTS

The second philosophical objection follows from the first. This objection asserts that it is impossible for the Mormon doctrine of eternal progression to be true even if we assume that the past series of events in time is infinite. There are at least three ways to show the implausibility of this Mormon Doctrine.

On Reaching Our Inevitable Fate

According to Mormon theology,[23] all beings have existed in some state or another and are progressing or moving toward their inevitable eternal fate. McConkie writes:

> Endowed with agency and subject to eternal laws, man began his progression and advancement in pre-existence, his ultimate goal being to attain a state of glory, honor, and exaltation like the Father of spirits.... This gradually unfolding course—a course that began in a past eternity and will continue in ages future—is frequently referred to as *eternal progression.*
> It is important to know, however, that for the overwhelming majority of mankind, eternal progression has very definite limitations. In the full sense, eternal progression is enjoyed only by those who receive exaltation.[24]

But if the past series of events in time is infinite, we should have all reached our inevitable fate by now. The Mormon philosopher cannot say that there has not been enough time for this to have occurred, simply because his own metaphysic affirms that an infinite time has already occurred. One cannot ask for more time than an infinite. But since none of us has reached his inevitable fate, whether it be godhood or another celestial reward or punishment, it is apparent that the past series of events in time cannot be infinite as Mormon metaphysics teaches. The Mormon may argue against this argument by saying that prior to our spirits being organized our intelligences were in a non-progressive state. But this does not really answer the problem for two reasons. First, an infinite past also implies that there has certainly been enough time for all the intelligences to have been organized even if there were an infinite number of them. That is, there is a one-to-one correspondence between each moment in the infinite past and each intelligence, and there always has existed at least one god who is doing his duty of organizing, since that is what Mormon gods do (see note 25). And since Mormon theology also teaches that some of us will become gods of our own planets and will organize spirits from pre-existent intelligences in order to populate these planets, and since the future is potentially infinite, obviously there should currently exist an infinite number of intelligences that have not yet been organized.[25] Hence, the paradox remains. Second, if the primal intelligences were in a non-progressive state prior to their organization, then they were in that state for an infinite number of moments. But then one would run into the problem of crossing an infinite which we discussed above: since it is impossible to cross an infinite, how could a primal intelligence have crossed an infinite number of moments to reach that one moment when it was organized?

On an Infinite Number of Gods and an Infinite Number of Intelligences

There is another variation on this problem: Given what we know about Mormon metaphysics, at any point in the infinite past all the intelligences should be "used up." Consider the following. The Mormon must admit that there currently exists an infinite number of gods—primal intelligences who have reached their fullest maturity—since once a being becomes a god, he never ceases to exist. For if any god, X, had a cause which was another god, W, and that god had a cause which was another god, V, etc..., then an infinite series is generated and all its parts are still in existence. Hence, there currently exists an infinite number of gods. From this analysis it follows that for any point in the time-line there would exist an infinite number of gods, since at any point in the time-line the same analysis could be performed. And since according to Mormon metaphysics the gods are always in the process of taking primal intelligences and putting them on the path of eternal progression, therefore, at any one time each god is starting a primal intelligence on the path of eternal progression. But since all infinites are equal, if there are an infinite number of primal intelligences, each god could be matched to a primal intelligence, which means that all the primal intelligences would be "used up." In other words, since each one of the gods in the infinite set of gods would be matched with each one of the intelligences in the infinite set of intelligences, there never was a point on the time-line when there was a remaining intelligence which could be put on the path of eternal progression. Therefore, based on this argument, the Mormon view of eternal progression is internally incoherent.

In summary, our first two objections based on the Mormon doctrine of eternal progression show that the past must be finite in order for the doctrine to be coherent. But since an infinite past is the metaphysical foundation on which Mormon theology is built, the Mormon doctrine of eternal progression is incoherent.

On an Infinite Number of Remaining Intelligences

Mormon philosopher Blake Ostler has brought out another philosophical problem with the doctrine of eternal progression:

> Even so, the doctrine of personal eternalism raises problems for Mormon thought. If the number of intelligences is infinite, then an infinite number of intelligences will remain without the chance to progress by further organization. If, on the other hand, the number of intelligences is finite the eternal progression of gods resulting from begetting spirits must one day cease. Either way, the dilemma remains.[26]

The first horn of Ostler's dilemma claims that if we assume for the sake of argument that there has always existed an infinite number of intelligences and that there are currently a remaining number of intelligences which have yet to be organized (which Mormonism must assume if our own possible godhoods will produce spirit-children, although our first two critiques of eternal progression show that this assumption is incoherent), this number of remaining intelligences would still be infinite. For if one subtracts either a finite number or an infinite portion of an infinite number (e.g., half of an infinite set) from an infinite number, one does not literally subtract from an infinite number. For example, Craig asks us to consider a library with an infinite number of books:

> Suppose we loan out book number one. Isn't there now one fewer books in the collection? Let's loan out all the odd-numbered books. We have loaned out an infinite number of books, and yet mathematicians would say there are no fewer books in the collection.[27]

Hence, if the first horn of Ostler's dilemma is true, then an infinite number of intelligences will never even have an opportunity to progress to godhood. This means that the Mormon universe is fundamentally irrational, for this view admits that there exists an infinite number of beings who exist with no purpose and for no reason whatsoever. A Mormon can always respond by saying that this is simply the nature of the Mormon universe, a universe for which no rational being is responsible, and we must simply learn to live with it. But in admitting that there currently exists an infinite number of beings who exist with no purpose and for no reason whatsoever, the Mormon falls prey to both our critique of finitistic theology in chapter 4 and our next objection in this chapter—the impossibility of an actual infinite number of things in the material universe. If, however, the other horn of

Ostler's dilemma is true—that there exist only a finite number of intelligences—then eternal progression will someday cease, and should have already ceased if the past is infinite (as we noted in our above critique). But given an infinite future of gods and worlds, there must be an infinite number of intelligences for the Mormon scheme to work. But now we are back to the problems that follow from claiming that there exists an infinite number of intelligences. It seems that no matter how the doctrine of eternal progression is approached (whether our way or Ostler's), it seems to be fundamentally irrational.

THE IMPOSSIBILITY OF AN ACTUAL INFINITE NUMBER OF THINGS IN THE MATERIAL WORLD

As we have already seen in chapter 2, Mormon theology assumes the existence of an infinity large universe with an infinite number of things in it, such as gods and pre-existent intelligences. Of course, if the Mormon denies that there exist an infinite number of gods and pre-existent intelligences, then he has the problem of reconciling a finite number of these beings with an infinite past. For if the beings are a finite number and the past is infinite, then it follows that there was a time when no gods existed (which Joseph Smith denies)[28] or there will be or has been a time when no more pre-existent intelligences can become gods. At any rate, in order for Mormonism to remain internally consistent it seems that it must teach that there is something infinite in an infinity large universe.

But there is good philosophical reason to believe that the existence of an actual infinite number of things in the material world is impossible. Now an *actual* infinite should be distinguished from a *potential* infinite. For example, consider this line:

1	2	3	4	5	6

The length of this line is divided into six segments. Assuming that each segment equals an inch, this line is six inches long. Hence, it is not actually infinite, although it is *potentially* infinite insofar as one can in-principle keep dividing the line into smaller segments infinitely. For instance, if one tried to travel this six inch segment by crossing half the distance one has to cross in order to reach the end, one will never reach the end. Such a journey is potentially infinite. Let each vertical line on the horizontal line symbolize the end of each journey half-way to the end:

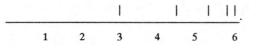

Since one never reaches the end of this line, the *potential* infinite is just that—potential. In fact, a potential infinite is not really infinite, it is *indefinite*. As Craig puts it, "A potential infinite is a collection that is increasing without limit but is at all times finite."[29] Now when mathematicians talk about an actual infinite they mean a set of numbers that is unlimited in its members. They do not mean a set that is potentially infinite. And when they discuss the actual infinite, it is strictly theoretical. They do not discuss a particular infinite number of apples, dogs, cars, or indicted clergymen. They discuss a set of numbers that refer to nothing in the empirical world. For once one tries to apply the infinite to the real world—the world of empirical objects and things—all sorts of absurdities develop. Given this fact, the belief that there can exist an infinite number of things in the empirical world, which the Mormons believe, must be rejected. Our argument can be put in this way:

> 1. It is impossible that an actual infinite can exist in the real world.
> 2. Mormon metaphysics, which is entailed by its concept of God, teaches that there currently exists an actual infinite number of things in the real world.
> 3. Therefore, the Mormon concept of God is incoherent.

The disputable premise in this argument is the first one. If this premise is true, or more likely to be true than not, the conclusion follows since the argument is deductively valid. Hence, given the truth of (1), our argument is sound. A number of examples serve to show that (1) is true. First, if it is possible that an actual infinite could exist in the real world, there could exist an actually infinite set of baseball cards. Imagine that this collection can be equally divided into two types of cards, American League and National League. If we are told that the American League cards are equal in number to the National League cards, we would readily agree. But what would be our reaction if we are told that the total number of American

League cards is equal to the total number of cards of both leagues combined? ($A + N = A$ and $A + N = N$). At first we would probably be a little suspicious, but we would have to admit that it is true. For just as the infinite set of all natural numbers (which includes both odd [O] and even [E] numbers), U (1,2,3...), is equal to the infinite set of all odd natural numbers, O (1,3,5...) (that is, $O = U = O + E$), an infinite set of all baseball cards (both American and National League) would be equal to an infinite set of all American League cards ($A = A + N$). That is, to add to or subtract from an infinite number does not alter the total number of an infinite set. With this absurdity in mind, can anyone really believe that an actual infinite can exist in the material world?

To continue with this example, imagine that every baseball card in this collection is numbered. But being an actual infinite, each possible natural number is located on each card in the collection. And since this collection is infinite, there are no numbers left, all of them have been taken. Hence, since every possible number has been assigned to every card in our collection, it is impossible to add to this collection. Yet, if all of a sudden we gave away the cards of Dwight Gooden and Wade Boggs to a desperate New York Met/Boston Red Sox fan, our collection would still contain the same number of entities; for we would still have an infinite set of cards and every number would be taken.

Other examples can be used to demonstrate the absurdity of having an actual infinite in the material world. Citing an example used by Craig, to which we have already alluded, Moreland writes:

> Imagine a library with an actually infinite number of books. Suppose further that there is an infinite number of red books and an infinite number of black books in the library. Does it really make sense to say that there are as many black books in the library as there are red and black books together? Surely not. Furthermore, I could withdraw all the black books and not change the total holdings in the library. Let us also assume that each book has an actual infinite number of pages. There would be just as many pages in the first book in the library as there are in the entire, infinite collection. If someone read the first book, she would have read just as many pages as someone who read every page of every book in the library![30]

Moreland presents another example originally offered by Bertrand Russell:[31]

> The example is about a person, Tristam Shandy, who writes his autobiography so slowly that it takes a whole year to write just one day of his life. If he lives an actually infinite number of days, he will alleged-

ly be able to complete his autobiography. This is because the set of all the days in his life can be put into one-to-one correspondence with the set of all his years. But does this really make sense? It would seem that the longer he lives the further behind he would get.[32]

Finally, imagine the absurd conclusions one arrives at when thinking about the consequences of the actual infinite for Mormon metaphysics. First, if there are an actually infinite number of pre-existent intelligences, then if there were half as many, there would be as many as there are now. Second, if there are an infinite number of gods, then if there were, let's say, ten less gods than there are now, then there would still be an infinite number of gods. In fact, if there were 10 zillion less gods, there would still be an infinite number. Since these conclusions are patently absurd, Mormon metaphysics, which is entailed by the Mormon concept of God, is absurd. Hence, since an actual infinite cannot exist in the material world, the Mormon concept of God is at best false or at worst incoherent.

Although the above puzzles have convinced many that an actual infinite cannot exist in the material world, some are not persuaded. Moreland has outlined three major objections to our defense of premise one.[33] First, it has been argued that since it is possible for mathematicians to talk coherently about infinite sets, we must alter our world-view and admit the possibility of an actual infinite existing in the real world. We believe that this objection is unsuccessful. As Moreland points out, "The mere presence of a generally accepted theory of mathematics, says nothing, by itself, about anything in the real world of entities."[34]

We believe that this first objection can be put in the following argument-outline:

1. An actual infinite is mathematically possible.
2. Therefore, an actual infinite can exist in the material world.

The problem with this argument is that the conclusion does not follow from the premise. Only if the following premise is added does the argument achieve deductive validity:

1$_a$.Whatever is mathematically possible can exist in the material world.

But this premise is not obviously true. In fact, we can argue that it is false precisely because of the paradoxes that are generated when one applies an actual infinite to the material world. For this reason, and the fact that this premise has not been adequately supported by argument (it is merely

assumed to be true, which makes the whole argument in a sense question-begging), we have been given no compelling reason to dispense with our view that an actual infinite cannot
exist in the material world.

The second objection claims that our argument amounts to saying that the actual infinite is impossible in the real world because the rules that usually function with finite sets do not do so when applied to the actual infinite—such as, "a part of a set is not equal to the whole." Hence, we are merely faulting an infinite set for not being a finite set.[35]

Moreland believes that this objection has some force but ultimately fails. In order to understand Moreland's conclusion, let us look at two parallel cases he cites. The first case involves the age-old philosophical debate between realists and nominalists over the existence of universals (e.g., blueness, humanness, wisdom, goodness, etc.). Realists believe that universals are real entities, while nominalists believe that universals do not exist but are merely *names* that we attach to the attributes of particulars, e.g., "The Subaru and the dress are both light blue." Since universals are supposedly real entities that exist in more than place at the same time (e.g., individual humans participate in "humanness," two particular red cars participate in "redness"), nominalists argue that realism is wrong because it is impossible for a thing to be in more than location simultaneously. Realists believe that this objection is unsuccessful because it is faulting a universal for not being a particular. But the nature of a universal is such that it is *supposed* to be in more than place at the same time. Just as the defender of the actual infinite believes that our error lies in the fact that we are faulting an infinite set for not being a finite set, the realist is arguing that the nominalist is in error for faulting a universal for not being a particular.

The second parallel case involves an individual who argues that a square circle (or a "married-bachelor" or "brother who is an only child") is impossible because the properties of such a "thing" are internally contradictory. A square circle apologist might reply that this argument is in error because the arguer is faulting an internally contradictory thing for not being internally consistent. We agree with Moreland that this reply will not work:

> First, the concepts *square* and *circle* are no longer functioning in a clear, normal way. If they were, then it would seem intuitive that these attributes could not be conjoined in one object. They seem to exclude each other. Second, the defender of the square circle has not given us reasons which are sufficient to warrant overturning our basic intuitions about reality.[36]

This differs radically from the realist/nominalist debate. Those familiar with the debate realize that the realist presents a number of arguments to justify the reasonableness in believing in the existence of universals. He defends a broad and sophisticated theory of existence which he believes justifies the realist notion that a universal can exist in more than one location simultaneously.[37] The square-circle apologist does nothing of the sort, but merely assumes the truth of his belief.

From these two cases, Moreland concludes that "it seems that the defender of the actual infinite is more like the defender of square circles than the defender of universals."[38] He explains:

> [The defender of the actual infinite] argues that one should accept the principle that a part can be equal to a whole and thus the puzzles [i.e., the infinite set of baseball cards, the library with an infinite set of books] should be rejected. [We are arguing] that a whole is greater than any of its parts and thus the puzzles argue against the existence of an actual infinite. There do not seem to be sufficient, independent reasons for accepting an actual infinite with its unusual properties. As has been pointed out, the mere presence of the mathematics of infinity is insufficient, and I know of no other reason which sufficiently justifies the acceptance of infinite sets. Further, the lack of justification becomes more troublesome when we realize that terms like "part," "add," or "subtract" are being used in such an odd way in connection with the actual infinite that this usage should be rejected because it lacks sufficient justification. How can something still be a part of a whole if it equals that whole? How can members be "added to" or "subtracted from" a set without increasing or decreasing its members?[39]

The defender of the actual infinite has not been able to justify *why* what intuitively makes no sense when one applies the actual infinite to reality—"the part is equal to the whole"—*ipso facto* makes sense simply because an actual infinite set is by nature different than a finite set. Therefore, it follows that this second objection fails to eliminate the force of the absurd consequences of the actual infinite.

A third objection is defended by Sorabji.[40] He argues that if he can show that terms like "subtraction," "addition," and "part" can be sufficiently clarified when applied to an actual infinite, then the absurd consequences of applying an actual infinite to reality are not really that absurd and hence are not successful in showing the impossibility of an actual infinite. Sorabji believes that he can adequately clarify the principle that a part can be equal to its whole so that this principle ceases to be a problem.

Sorabji asks us to suppose that there are two lines which extend from the present moment and traverse the infinite past. Line A contains an actual infinite number of days, while line B contains an actual infinite number of years.

infinite past (in the direction of the "far end")

A... ←———·———·———·———·———·———·———·———·
    1/1/91 1/2/91 1/3/91 1/4/91 1/5/91 1/6/91 1/7/91 1/8/91

infinite past (in the direction of the "far end")

B... ←———·———·———·———·———·———·———·———·
      1984   1985   1986   1987   1988   1989   1990   1991

Writes Sorabji, "I can now explain the sense in which the column of past days is not larger than the column of past years: it will not *stick out beyond the far end of* the other column, since neither column has a far end."[41] Now in the case of the infinite set of baseball cards, C, one is tempted to think that if one adds another card to the collection, one of the cards currently in the set will have to be eliminated to make room for the new card. But since, according to Sorabji, there is no "far end" (that is, no limit to the infinite set), the number of cards will not "stick out" beyond the far end of the line. For this reason, Sorabji argues that $C + 1$ is an infinite set which contains an additional member which C, an infinite set, does not. But this only means that $C + 1$ contains something *beside* what C contains; it does not mean that $C + 1$ contains members *beyond* C. Hence, it is possible to "add" another card to the collection although there would still be an infinite number of cards. Naturally, the same reasoning would justify the use of the terms "subtraction" and "part" when discussing the actual infinite.

There are at least three problems with Sorabji's reasoning. First, he clearly begs the question. He assumes the existence of two actually infinite states of affairs, lines A and B, and then argues that he can imagine adding to them by making a distinction between *beyond* and *besides*. But the very point under question is whether an actual infinite can exist. Merely asserting that it does exist does not solve any of the problems. Suppose someone who is defending the coherence of believing in square circles argues, "Imagine that there exist two square circles and a merchant is selling them in his store. Hence, a square circle can exist." This is clearly question begging. Sorabji commits the same fallacy, although it is less obvious.

Second, Sorabji's distinction between *beyond* and *besides* does not really solve any of the problems of the actual infinite really existing, but rather accentuates the problems. For instance, if $C + 1$, an infinite set, has one member *besides* the number contained in C, an infinite set, how are the absurd consequences of a real actual infinite alleviated by simply asserting that the total number of members of $C + 1$ does not go *beyond* the total number of members of C? The fact that $C + 1$ can have one more member than C and yet not go beyond C in its total number of members *is* absurd. This is *precisely* why we believe it is impossible to have an actual infinite in the material world.

Third, Craig believes that "Sorabji's own illustration of the columns of past years and days is a little disquieting."[42] He explains:

> If we divide the [actual infinite] columns into foot-long segments and mark one column as the years [line B] and the other as the days [line A], then one column is as long as the other and yet for every foot-length segment in the column of years, 365 segments of equal length are found in the column of days![43]

How can such a situation exist? How can A be equal to B although A has 365 members for every one of B's? Answering this question by asserting that the lines do not have far ends where one can stick out further than the other, as Sorabji asserts, simply begs the question. For it is *precisely* because there are no far ends to these lines that the absurd consequences of an actual infinite result. We believe that Craig is right when he says that "these paradoxical results can be avoided only if such actually infinite collections can exist only in the imagination, not in reality."[44]

Sorabji's analysis does not sufficiently clarify the notion of an actual infinite so as to solve the paradoxes that result in applying the actual infinite to reality. As Moreland writes, "He [Sorabji] merely asserts its [the actual infinite's] existence by setting up the example the way he does. But the problematic puzzles appear all over again."[45] In summary, it seems that the three objections to the first premise of our argument fail to overturn its force. Hence, the belief that there currently exists an infinite number of things in the material universe, which is entailed by the Mormon concept of God, is at best false and at worst incoherent. Therefore, the Mormon concept of God is incoherent.

THE IMPOSSIBILITY OF ACHIEVING OMNISCIENCE IN TIME AND SPACE

We saw in chapter 2 that Mormonism teaches that God *achieves* omniscience sometime in his progression to godhood. We have also seen that the God of Mormonism is subject to the limits of time and space. Furthermore, in this chapter we have seen that Mormonism teaches that there currently exists an infinite number of things in time and space. We will argue in this section that God's achieving of omniscience is inconsistent with (1) God being subject to the limits of time and space and (2) the existence of an infinite number of things in time and space.

Omniscience and the Limits of Time and Space

In their critique of process theology, Norman Geisler and William Watkins present an argument that is applicable to the Mormon concept of God:

> They believe [both Mormons and process theologians] that God comprehends the whole universe at one time. Yet they also believe that God is limited to space and time. Anything limited to space and time cannot think any faster than the speed of light, which takes billions of years to cross the universe at about 186,000 miles per second. However, it seems quite impossible that a mind which takes this amount of time to think its way around the universe could simultaneously comprehend and direct the whole universe. On the other hand, if God's mind transcends the universe of space and time, and instantly and simultaneously comprehends the whole of it, then this is not a panentheistic [or Mormon] view of God but a theistic view.[46]

We can add to this observation that the Mormon God has a body, and hence, a brain, which we assume functions like our brains except in a more advanced way.[47] Yet if it is really a brain, it must have certain electrical impulses when it is functioning. But electrical impulses cannot go faster than the speed of light. Hence, the Mormon God cannot be omniscient in the limited sense (i.e., eliminating knowledge of the future) of knowing everything that is currently occurring (the present) and that has occurred (the past) in the universe.[48] At any rate, if God is limited in time and space, regardless of whether his brain is in any way like our's, it would be impossible for him to know everything instantly and simultaneously without transcending time and space. Our argument can be put in the following form:

1. The Mormon God is limited by time and space.
2. What is limited by time and space cannot transcend time and space.
3. Therefore, the Mormon God cannot transcend time and space.
4. Knowing everything instantly and simultaneously involves exceeding the limits of time and space.
5. The Mormon God knows everything instantly and simultaneously.
6. Therefore, the Mormon God exceeds (i.e., transcends) the limits of time and space.
7. Therefore, given 3 and 6, the Mormon God both transcends and cannot transcend the limits of time and space.
8. Therefore, the Mormon concept of God is internally inconsistent and incoherent.

Premises 4 and 5 may be disputed by Mormon scholars, but we don't see how. For instance, as we noted in both chapter 2 and in note 48 in this chapter, Mormon scholars teach that God currently knows everything. This clearly entails premise 5: God knows everything that is going on everywhere in the infinite universe at this moment, i.e., he knows everything instantly and simultaneously. Yet, as Geisler and Watkins have pointed out, this would involve God exceeding the limits of the physical universe, which is clearly denied by Mormon theology.

A Mormon scholar could deny premise 4 by arguing that it is conceivable for a being to know everything instantly and simultaneously without exceeding the limits of time and space. He could argue that it is natural for God's thoughts to exceed the speed of light, but it would be a natural speed that our minds have not yet conceived. Therefore, it is possible that God can know everything instantly and simultaneously. But there are at least two problems with this argument. First, it still does *not* follow from the Mormon's newly constructed premises that God knows everything instantly and simultaneously. For even if God's thought processes naturally exceed the speed of light, they must have *some* speed. Hence, no matter how fast God's thoughts are, there would still be a period of time between an event occurring on the furthest edges of the universe and God knowing that the event has occurred. Therefore, for some period of time, God would *not* be omniscient in the sense of knowing everything that is currently occurring or has occurred. Second, suppose the Mormon further clarifies this argument by arguing that there is no process by which God attains knowledge of all events; He simply knows things *immediately* in the sense that there is no time between an event occurring in the furthest regions of the universe and God knowing it. Besides the fact that it begs the question, how does this proposal

differ from the classical view of God, which teaches that God knows everything immediately precisely because He is not limited by time and space?
Therefore, only if the Mormon incorporates the classical view of God's
knowledge can his view be rescued.

Achieving Omniscience of an Infinite Number of Things in Time and Space

We have seen that Mormon theology teaches that becoming a god involves an eternal *progression*. Explaining this in the life of an individual,
McConkie writes that "during his earth life he gains a mortal body, receives
experience in earthly things, and prepares for a future eternity after the
resurrection when he will continue to gain knowledge and intelligence. (D.
& C. 130:18-19.)."[49] The God of this world went through the same process
until he reached a point at which he is "not progressing in knowledge, truth,
virtue, wisdom, or any of the attributes of godliness."[50] In other words, God's
progress entails an increase from finite knowledge until he reaches the *point*
of omniscience, infinite knowledge. We believe that the idea of God progressing to the point at which his knowledge is infinite (omniscience) is
incoherent. Our argument can be put in the following way:

> 1. A being of limited knowledge gaining in knowledge entails
> the increasing of a finite number.
> 2. Starting from a finite number it is impossible to count to
> infinity.
> 3. The Mormon view of eternal progression entails that a
> being of limited knowledge gains in knowledge until his knowledge is
> infinite (remember, the Mormon universe contains an infinite
> number of things).
> 4. Therefore, the Mormon view is impossible, for it is impos-
> sible, given 1, 2, and 3, for eternal progression to entail that a being
> of limited knowledge gains knowledge until his knowledge is infinite.
> 5. The Mormon doctrine of eternal progression is entailed by
> the Mormon concept of God.
> 6. Therefore, the Mormon concept of God is incoherent.

Let us examine each one of these premises. According to the
Mormon view, all beings, prior to attaining godhood, are limited in knowledge (see D. & C. 130:18-19). Hence every being, prior to achieving godhood, regardless of how much each knows in comparison to the other, pos-

sesses a finite amount of knowledge. And every piece of knowledge gained by any one of these beings amounts to an increase of a finite number. Therefore, premise one seems correct: a being of limited knowledge gaining in knowledge entails the increasing of a finite number.

Premise two states that starting from a finite number it is impossible to count to infinity. We have already seen earlier in this chapter that it is impossible to traverse an infinite (see pp. 54-59). Hence, it follows that it is impossible to count to infinity. Even those philosophers, such as Sorabji,[51] who believe that it is possible to traverse an infinite past because it has no starting point, agree that it is impossible to count to infinity if one has a starting point. For one will never arrive at infinity by adding one member after another, since when starting a count from a finite number there is no place in the count at which one passes from a finite to an infinite number of members. To cite an example we employed earlier in this chapter, one can never travel an infinite distance. If you were to drive on Interstate 15 from Las Vegas to Salt Lake City with 450 miles to cross, there is no doubt, all things being equal, that you would eventually arrive in Salt Lake. However, if you were to drive on an interstate from Vegas to Salt Lake with an infinite number of miles to cross, you would never arrive in Salt Lake. This is because it is impossible to complete an infinite by adding one member (or one mile, or one bit of knowledge) after another. For if you did arrive in Salt Lake it would only prove that your journey was finite, not infinite; you can always drive further north to Ogden or Pocatello, Idaho. To use another example we employed earlier. Consider the following line:

```
                    |          |     |   | |.
_____
    1       2       3       4       5       6
```

The vertical lines on this line represent each journey taken half-way to the end. As we noted earlier, if one covers only half the distance to the end every time one moves on one's way to trying to reach the end, one will never reach the end of the line. For this reason, we say that this line is *potentially* infinitely divisible. This example serves to illustrate why one can never count to infinity. For to count to infinity is like covering only half the distance to the end every time one moves on one's way to trying to reach the end of the line. No matter how many times one travels half-way, one will never reach the end. In like manner, no matter for how long one counts, one will never count to infinity. Therefore, it is impossible to count to infinity when starting from a finite number.

The third premise—the Mormon view of eternal progression entails that a being of limited knowledge gains in knowledge until his knowledge is infinite—is clearly taught in the Mormon writings. This view is succinctly put by Joseph Smith:

> Here, then, is eternal life—to know the only wise and true God; and you have to learn how to be gods yourselves, and to be kings and priests to God, the same as all gods have done before you, namely, by going from *one small degree to another, and from a small capacity to a great one; from grace to grace, from exaltation to exaltation, until you attain the resurrection of the dead and are able to dwell in everlasting burnings, and to sit in glory, as do those who sit enthroned in everlasting power*.... When you climb up a ladder, you must begin at the bottom, and ascend step by step, until you arrive at the top; and so it is with the principles of the gospel—you must begin with the first, and go on until you learn all the principles of exaltation.[52] (emphasis ours).

Therefore, premise 4 follows from premises 1, 2 and 3 , and linking premise 4 with premise 5 (a foundational belief of Mormon theism), our final conclusion follows: the Mormon concept of God is incoherent.

Someone may respond to this argument by arguing that the Mormon God receives his infinite knowledge from his God all at once when he reaches a particular point in his progression. Hence, there is no problem in starting from finite knowledge and arriving at infinite knowledge. But we believe that there are at least three problems with this response.

First, there is no evidence that this is the Mormon view of eternal progression. As we have seen, the Mormon literature seems to teach that one progresses from "one small degree to another." Second, even if one did receive one's infinite knowledge all at once, an embarrassing problem would remain: eternal *progression* makes no progress. For once one receives the infinite knowledge, the prior progression from "one small degree to another" becomes totally unnecessary. Since the notion of progression entails an increase from one state to another (e.g., "After driving 100 miles in 90 minutes, it is accurate to say that we have made progress in our trip to Salt Lake City."), and we know that one cannot progress to infinity by starting from a finite point, this view of eternal progression makes any "progression" unessential to the achieving of infinite knowledge. In other words, one's "progress" prior to the reception of infinite knowledge was getting one nowhere. But since eternal progression is essential to achieving Godhood, this view runs counter to accepted Mormon teaching. And third, by saying that the Mormon God receives his infinite knowledge from his God all at once, the Mormon thinker does not *really* address the issue of explaining how God acquired his knowledge; he merely places the problem on the shoulders of a more distant God, who himself must appeal to his Father-God to explain his own acquisition of omniscience. And obviously, this exercise of finding an explanation for a God's knowledge goes on infinitely. But there is a serious problem in appealing to an endless series of contingent beings as an explanation for all contingent beings, namely: If being A does not have the sufficient reason for his omniscience in the being who formed him, being B, but requires other prior conditions (the former of B, C, and the former of C, D, *ad infinitum*), and so on forever, then the conditions for the omniscience of any one of the beings in the series are never fulfilled and can never be fulfilled in principle. It follows from this that none of the beings in the Mormon universe could ever actually have infinite knowledge (omniscience), since the necessary conditions for such knowledge could never be fulfilled.

NOTES FOR CHAPTER THREE

1. For example, see W. Norris Clarke, S.J., *The Philosophical Approach to God* (Winston-Salem, NC: Wake Forest University Press, 1979); Norman L. Geisler, "Process Theology," in *Tensions in Contemporary Theology*, eds. Stanley N. Gundry and Alan F. Johnson (Chicago: Moody Press, 1976), pp. 237-284; Ronald Nash, *The Concept of God* (Grand Rapids, MI: Zondervan, 1983); Alvin Plantinga, *Does God Have a Nature?* (Milwaukee: Marquette University Press, 1980); Alvin Plantinga, *God Freedom, and Evil* (Grand Rapids, MI: Eerdmans, 1974); and Richard Swinburne, *The Coherence of Theism* (Oxford: Clarendon, 1977).

2. For example, see Gary James Bergera, ed., *Line Upon Line: Essays in Mormon Doctrine* (Salt Lake City: Signature Books, 1989); Sterling McMurrin, *The Philosophical Foundations of Mormon Theology* (Salt Lake City: University of Utah Press, 1959); Sterling M. McMurrin, *The Theological Foundations of the Mormon Religion* (Salt Lake City: University of Utah Press, 1965); Blake Ostler, "The Mormon Concept of God," *Dialogue: A Journal of Mormon Thought* 17 (Summer 1984): 65-93; David Lamont Paulsen, *The Comparative Coherency of Mormon (Finitistic) and Classical Theism* (Ann Arbor, MI: University Microfilms, 1975); Kent Robson, "Omnis on the Horizon," *Sunstone* 8 (July-August 1983): 21-23; Kent Robson, "Time and Omniscience in Mormon Theology," *Sunstone* 5 (May-June 1980): 17-23; and O. Kendall White, Jr., *Mormon Neo-orthodoxy: A Crisis Theology* (Salt Lake City: Signature Books, 1987), pp. 57-67.

3. Joseph Fielding Smith, *Doctrines of Salvation*, 3 vols. (Salt Lake City: Bookcraft, 1959), 1: 12.

4. *Journal of Discourses, by Brigham Young, President of the Church of Jesus Christ of Latter-day Saints, His Two Counsellors, the Twelve Apostles, and Others*, 26 vols., reported by G.D. Watt (Liverpool: F.D. Richards, 1854-1886), 5: 19.

5. Bruce McConkie, *Mormon Doctrine*, 2nd ed. (Salt Lake City: Bookcraft, 1979), p. 77.

6. White, *Mormon Neo-orthodoxy*, p. 61.

7. Craig has presented these arguments in their most detailed form in his *The Kalam Cosmological Argument* (New York: Barnes and Noble, 1979). A popular version of his arguments can found in his *The Existence of God and the Beginning of the Universe* (San Bernardino, CA: Here's Life, 1979) J.P. Moreland defends Craig's arguments in his *Scaling the Secular City* (Grand Rapids: Baker, 1987), pp. 18-42.

8. Craig, *The Existence of God*, p. 49.

9. Moreland, *Scaling*, p. 29.

10. Thomas Aquinas, "On the Eternity of the World against the Grumblers," as found in *An Aquinas Reader*, ed. and intro. Mary T. Clark (Garden City, NY: Image Books, 1972), pp. 178-185; and Thomas Aquinas, *Summa Theologica*, I, 46, as found in *Introduction to St. Thomas Aquinas*, ed. and intro. Anton C. Pegis (New York: The Modern Library, 1948), pp. 246-258.

It should be noted that Aquinas himself did not believe in eternal creation. He is merely asserting that since there is no clear philosophical proof against it, the Christian can only believe in a beginning of time on the basis of faith, as he does with the doctrine of the Trinity. See *Summa Theologica*, I, 46. 2.

11. Aquinas, "Eternity of the World," pp. 180-181.

12. James Sadowsky, S.J., review of *The Kalam Cosmological Argument*, by William Lane Craig, *International Philosophical Quarterly* 21 (June 1981): 222. Of course, this "purely static condition" would be a condition completely unknown to contemporary science, and would be incapable of moving from inaction to action without a necessary and sufficient condition for it do so.

13. Aquinas, *Summa Theologica*, I, 46. 2.

14. Bernardino Bonansea, O.F.M., "The Impossibility of Creation from Eternity According to St. Bonaventure," *Proceedings of the American Catholic Philosophical Association* 48 (1974): 124.

15. Sadowsky cites another Thomistic objection: "Aquinas has a curious objection: he denies that an eternity of past events constitutes a completed infinity on the grounds that since the past no longer exists, it is not an actual infinity. But it is logically possible for each event to have left a permanent trace and that would surely involve the consummated infinite." (Sadowsky, review of *Kalam*, p. 222). Because this objection deals with the impossibility of the existence of an actual infinite number of things rather than an actual infinite number of events in the past, it does not seriously challenge our argument. We chose to deal only with the two which really pose a threat.

16. William Wainwright, review of *The Kalam Cosmological Argument* by William Lane Craig, *Nous* 16 (May 1982): 328-334; and J.L. Mackie, *The Miracle of Theism* (Oxford: Clarendon, 1982), p. 93.

17. Mackie, *Miracle*, p. 93.

18. Moreland, *Scaling*, p. 31.

19. Richard Sorabji, *Time, Creation and the Continuum* (Ithaca, NY: Cornell University Press, 1983), pp. 221-222.

20. Moreland, *Scaling*, p. 32.

21. *Ibid.*, pp. 31-32.

22. For detailed responses to these other objections, see William Lane Craig, "*Creatio ex nihilo*," in *Process Theology*, ed. Ronald Nash (Grand Rapids, MI: Baker Book House, 1987), pp. 163-166, and Moreland, *Scaling*, pp. 30-33.

Someone may ask why our criticism of an infinite regress does not hurt the God of classical theism who is said to be an eternal being. In response, Craig has written: "Prior to creation, there was no time at all, for time cannot exist unless there is change. God Himself is changeless [i.e., immutable]; otherwise you would find an infinite series of past events in His life, and we know that such an infinite series is impossible. So God is changeless, and hence, timeless prior to creation." (Craig, *The Existence of God*, p. 87). In other words, since there was no time or change prior to the beginning of the universe, and hence no series of events, there was no infinite series of past events in God's existence.

23. This is not to say that Mormons have always agreed with each other on the doctrine of pre-existence. In this book we are referring to the version of the doctrine which we believe is the one currently held by the leadership of the LDS church. For an excellent overview of the history of the doctrine of pre-existence, see Blake Ostler, "The Idea of Pre-Existence in the Development of Mormon Thought," *Dialogue: A Journal of Mormon Thought* 15 (Spring 1982): 59-78.

24. McConkie, *Mormon Doctrine*, pp. 238-239.

25. See Joseph Smith, *History of the Church of Jesus Christ of Latter-day Saints*, 7 vols., intro. and notes B.H. Roberts (Deseret Books, 1978), 6:305-312 (from now on, *HC*). That a Mormon god's natural duty is to produce spirit-children is confirmed by McConkie, who writes: "In a future eternity, *spirit children* will be born to exalted, perfected, glorified couples for whom the family unit continues. The very glory of exalted beings is to have 'fullness and continuation of their *seeds* forever and ever.' (D. & C. 132:19-25, 29-32; 131:1-4.)" (McConkie, *Mormon Doctrine*, p. 751.)

26. Ostler, "The Idea of Pre-existence," p. 74.

27. Craig, *Existence of God*, p. 45.

28. Joseph Smith seems to teach an infinite lineage of gods when he writes, "Hence, if Jesus had a Father, can we not believe that *He* had a Father also?...." (Smith, *DHC*, 6:476). Confirming this interpretation, a successor of Smith, President Joseph Fielding Smith writes that the "Prophet [Joseph Smith] taught that *our Father had a Father and so on*." (J.F. Smith, *Doctrines of Salvation*, 1:12). See also, McConkie, *Mormon Doctrine*, p. 577.

29. Craig, *The Existence of God*, p. 40.

30. Moreland, *Scaling*, p. 23.

31. Cited in Abraham Fraenkel, *Abstract Set Theory* (Amsterdam: North-Holland Publishing, 1961), p. 6.

32. Moreland, *Scaling*, p. 23.

33. *Ibid.*, pp. 24-28. Our critique of these three objections is for the most part derived from Moreland's critique.

34. *Ibid*, p. 24.

35. Fraenkel, *Abstract Set Theory*, p. 20; and Mackie, *Miracle of Theism*, pp. 92-95.

36. Moreland, *Scaling*, p. 26.

37. For a defense of realism, see J.P. Moreland, *Universals, Qualities, and Quality-Instances: A Defense of Realism* (Lanham, MD: University Press of America, 1985)

38. Moreland, *Scaling*, p. 26.

39. *Ibid.*

40. Sorabji, *Time, Creation, and the Continuum*, pp. 217-218.

41. *Ibid.*, p. 217.

42. Craig, "*Creatio ex nihilo*," pp. 160.

43. *Ibid.*, pp. 160-161.

44. *Ibid.*, p. 161.

45. Moreland, *Scaling*, p. 28.

46. Norman L. Geisler and William D. Watkins, *Worlds Apart*, 2nd. ed. (Grand Rapids, MI: Baker, 1989), p. 145.

47. Joseph Smith writes that "God himself was once as we are now, and is an exalted man, and sits enthroned in yonder heavens!.... I say, if you were to see him today, you would see him like a man in form—like yourselves in all the person, image, and very form as a man; for Adam was created in the very fashion, image and likeness of God, and received instruction from, and walked, talked and conversed with Him, as one man talks and communes with another." (*HC*, 6: 305).

48. McConkie writes of the Mormon God's scope of omniscience: "God is *omniscient*. (*Lectures on Faith*, pp. 9, 43-45, 50-51; *Doctrines of Salvation*, vol. 1, pp. 5-10.) *Omniscience* consists in having unlimited knowledge. God knows all things (2 Ne. 9:20; D. & C. 38:1-2; 88:7-13); possesses a 'fullness of truth, yea, even of all truth' (D. & C. 93:11,26); 'has all power, all wisdom, and all understanding' (Alma 26:35); is infinite in understanding (Ps. 147:2-5); co comprehends all things (Alma 26:35; D. & C. 88:41); and 'hath given a law unto all things.' (D. & C. 88:42).... Joseph Smith said: 'Without the knowledge of all things God would not be able to save any portion of his creatures;... *and if it were not for the idea existing in the minds of men that God had all knowledge it would be impossible for them to exercise faith in him.*'(*Lectures on Faith*, p. 44.)." (McConkie, *Mormon Doctrine*, p. 545)

49. *Ibid.*, p. 238.

50. *Ibid.*, p. 239. But McConkie does admit that God "is progressing in the sense that his creations increase, his dominions expand, his spirit offspring multiply, and more kingdoms are added to his domains." (*Ibid.*)

51. Sorabji, *Time, Space and the Continuum*, pp. 219-222.

52. *HC*, 6: 306-307.

4
DESIGN, NECESSITY AND THE MORMON GOD

Mormon apologists have given positive defenses of their concept of God. For instance, some Mormon philosophers, such as David Lamont Paulsen, argue that although the existence of the infinite God of classical theism does not seem to follow from the apparent design found in the universe (the teleological argument), the God of Mormon finite theism does. In this chapter we will critically examine this defense of Mormon theism and show why it reveals that Mormon theism is fundamentally irrational.

With any philosophical position, there always comes the question of whether or not it is true. And of course this involves the problem of justification: how we decide if a belief is true. Classical theism has traditionally used three types of arguments of which there are many variations: cosmological, ontological, and teleological, the latter which are also known as arguments from design. The defenders of finitistic theism have used various approaches to justify their beliefs, but of the three types of theistic argumentation, the third one, the argument from design, seems the most amenable to justifying a believe in a finite God. This is because most cosmological and ontological arguments arrive back at the concept of a logically necessary being, which we have shown is the God of classical theism. On the other hand, teleological arguments, for the most part, do not seem to lead to a necessary being, but to a designer or builder of this particular universe. Simply put, a teleological argument is an attempt to establish God's existence based on the apparent design and purpose found in the physical universe; that is, a purposeful and designed universe implies a purposer and designer. But there is no need to ascribe infinity or necessity to Him, but just enough power and intelligence to cause the universe to have the particular structure that it currently possesses. The argument from design has been long discussed by various philosophers, and is perhaps the most "intuitive" of the three traditional arguments, i.e., the one that is most obvious to most non-philosophers. Some contemporary non-Mormon thinkers argue that the teleological argument and finitistic theism seem to have a natural affinity. Take for example a recent sophisticated defense of the design argument by Sir Frederick Hoyle and Dr. N. Chandra Wickramasinghe, *Evolution From Space*.[1] In this book they defend, among other things, the concept of a type of finite God, arguing that life could not have happened by chance, but had to have been designed.

Prior to examining Paulsen's use of the argument from design, we will take a brief look at how the argument has been defended by two other finitistic philosophers, John Stuart Mill and Edgar Sheffield Brightman. The reason for this is that their arguments are used by Paulsen to corroborate his defense of Mormon theism. We will also discuss the process philosopher Charles Hartshorne. Although he does not (to our knowledge) defend the teleological argument, some of his views directly concern important aspects of the debate between finitistic and classical theism.

MILL, BRIGHTMAN, AND THE ARGUMENT FROM DESIGN

Mill presented his argument for design in three essays which he wrote near the end of his life. They are *Nature*, *The Utility of Religion*, and *Theism*. The most detailed examination of the teleological argument comes in the last of these three essays. Mill's basic idea, and the one that he used to defend finitistic theism, is that there is evidence of intelligence and design in the universe which inclines one to think that there was a God behind the construction of the world. But there are also many evils and poorly designed things in nature that incline one to think that the universe was not designed. Mill's solution to this riddle is that there is a finite God, good, wise, and powerful, but certainly not all-powerful, and perhaps not all-wise, who had partial control over the universe. To quote Mill:

> Certain qualities, it is alleged, are found to be characteristic of such things as are made by an intelligent mind for a purpose. The order of Nature, or some considerable parts of it, exhibit these qualities in a remarkable degree. We are entitled, from this great similarity in the effects, to infer similarity in the cause, and to believe that things which it is beyond the power of men to make, but which

resemble the works of man in all but power, must also have been made by Intelligence armed with a power greater than human.[2]

In defense of this interpretation of the universe, Mill examines the eye, and the general collection of parts which compose it and which must all work together so that a person or animal may possess sight. He writes:

> Sight, being fact not precedent but subsequent to the putting together of the organic structure of the eye, can only be connected with the production of that structure in the character of a final, not an efficient cause; that is, it is not Sight itself but an antecedent Idea of it, that must be the efficient cause. But this at once marks the origin as proceeding from an intelligent will.[3]

Mill is saying that the balance of probability lies in favor of there being an intelligent designer of nature, that is, a creator. There is, however, another side to this. Along with the marks of design, there is also an appalling amount of evil and misery in the world. Mill comments:

> Killing, the most criminal act recognized by human laws, Nature does once to every being that lives; and in a large proportion of cases, after protracted tortures such as only the greatest monsters whom we read of ever purposely inflicted on their living fellow-creatures.... All this, Nature does with the most supercilious disregard both of mercy and of justice, emptying her shafts upon the best and noblest indifferently with the meanest and worst....[4]

Mill presents three arguments to show that the creator of the world is not omnipotent. The first one is the one stated above, that no omnipotent and good being would create a world such as this world, with the vast amounts of pain and evil which we see around us. The second is that around us we see means-ends relationships, where there is in nature contrivances, means adapted to bring about an end. For example, food nourishes human beings. Mill argues that an omnipotent creator would have no need of a means, for he could create the ends directly. Since God could easily make it that human beings be nourished without food, He is an inefficient being.[5] The third argument that Mill uses against the omnipotence of the creator is that

> ... no cause is needed for the existence of that which has no beginning; and both Matter and Force (whatever metaphysical theory we may give of the one or the other) have had, so far as our experience can teach us, no beginning....[6]

Thus, Mill concludes that there is a creator of the world and that this creator may be all good, but that He is not all-powerful, and perhaps not omniscient either (Mill could not decide on omniscience). The reason that he decided that the Creator is good is that "there is a preponderance of evidence that the Creator desired the pleasure of his creatures and, hence, is benevolent."[7] Mill sacrifices the creator's omnipotence to save his goodness, a common refrain among finitisitc thinkers.

In sum, Mill thought that the preponderance of evidence favored an eternal creator who desired to construct an orderly universe, but was somewhat frustrated in his designs by the fact that matter and force, which are co-eternal with him, did not permit the construction of a perfect universe. At any rate, Mill thought the combined evidence of both order and disorder-evil made the hypothesis of finitistic theism the most probable. Mill never asserted that his God is logically necessary, but rather implied that his God is contingent.

The second thinker in finite theism, who has defended a teleological argument is Edgar Sheffield Brightman. Working in the tradition of idealism, Brightman came up with a theory of God which is similar to Mills' in some respects but different in others. Although personal idealism (personalism) isn't a very popular philosophical school at the present, Brightman and others like him have been extremely influential in American philosophy of religion. To quote Paulsen on Brightman:

> ...Brightman has been identified as the leading American advocate of personalism, a metaphysical viewpoint for which the person is the ontological ultimate and for which personality is, thus, the fundamental explanatory principle.[8]

As far as theism and the argument from design goes, Brightman concluded that

> the will of God is limited by nonrational conditions (the Given) within the divine nature that are neither created nor approved by that will. God maintains constant—and growing—although never complete—control of the Given.[9]

Thus for Brightman, the uncreated and partially uncontrollable entities that God has to contend with are in his own nature (called "the Given") in contrast to the eternal existence of matter and force that Mill theorized.

In support of his hypothesis, Brightman makes use of a number of arguments, including an appeal to religious experience and the existence of value and personality. Most relevant for use here, however, is his defense of the teleological argument. He contends that the rationality of the universe is evidence for the existence of a designing mind, but that the existence of evil and suffering count as evidence for a finitistic, as opposed to a classical, idea of God. Since Brightman supported a strictly empirical approach to philosophy, he tried to combine all the evidence of the universe into one coherent theory. It was his complaint against both the nontheists and the classical theists that they ignored half the evidence. On the argument from design he said:

> All evidence for *law and order* in a universe is also evidence for a personal mind at work in that universe. Strangely enough, the opposite has often been supposed to be the case. Anomalies, miracles, eccentricities, have been taken as evidence of a divine mind. But the law which shows what Sir James Jeans has called a divine mathematician at work is plainly evidence that is consistent with regarding the physical cosmos as the energizing of a rational mind. While order does not necessitate mind, mind necessitates order and order is coherent with mind.... All evidence for *purpose*, either *as a psychological fact* in man and other animals, *or as a biological or physiochemical* fact of objective adaptation of means to ends in nature... *or as a directive force in evolution*... is evidence for a personal God. While it is conceivable that the appearance of purpose may be caused by what has no purpose, the number of telic facts is so great that the appeal to accident or coincidence becomes less plausible as the evidence multiplies. That accident should produce as much purpose as actually exists would be no less than magical.[10]

Thus, Brightman finds that the apparent order and purpose in the universe is impossible to explain without the hypothesis of a designing mind. Of course, the other side of this is of course the problem of evil. Focusing on one aspect of that problem, evolution, Brightman comments:

> Thus the evidence of evolution is seemingly contradictory. It points toward purposeless waste and futility; and it points toward purposeful creation and value. Center on one half of the evidence, and you become an atheist. Center on the other half and you become a theistic absolutist.... It is an undeniable fact that law, creative evolution and purposive advance are revealed in evolution. It is equally undeniable that this purposive advance marches on in the presence of the difficulties of waste and purposeless facts.... The hypothesis which these facts force on us is that of a finite God. Let us suppose a creative and rational will at work within limitations not of its own making. Then the world of life as we see it is what would be expected if the

hypothesis is true; it appears to be the work of spirit in difficulty, but a spirit never conquered by the difficulties.... Such is the argument from evolution for belief in a finite God. It is the hypothesis which best "saves the appearance" of the good-and-evil of evolution.[11]

Thus, arguing from apparently contradictory data, Brightman comes to the conclusion that taking a middle position will do justice to all the facts.

MORMON THEISM AND THE ARGUMENT FROM DESIGN

In the most sophisticated application of the teleological argument by a finite theist, Paulsen uses the argument to show that Mormon theism is a better alternative to classical theism in explaining the design one finds in the universe. Paulsen starts out by admitting that the teleological argument has come under devastating attack, particularly by David Hume and Immanuel Kant. But, he goes on to say, their attacks really count as evidence against classical theism and for finitistic theism. Paulsen writes:

Coupled with this faulting of the argument, however, has been an acknowledgement by many of the argument's most vigorous critics that the evidence *does* provide support for the existence of a powerful and intelligent world-designer, or stated another way, that the hypothesis of a powerful and intelligent world-designer adequately and illuminatingly accounts for the teleological data.[12]

In support of this contention Paulsen quotes both Kant and Hume. Says Kant:

The utmost, therefore, that the argument can prove is an architect of the world who is always hampered by the adaptability of the materials in which he works, not a creator of the world whose idea everything is subject. This, however, is altogether inadequate to the lofty purpose which we have before our eyes, namely, the proof of an all-sufficient primordial being.[13]

Hume writes:

In many views of the universe, and of its parts, particularly the latter, the beauty and fitness of final causes strike us with such irresistible force that all objections appear (what I believe they really are) mere cavils and sophisms; nor can we then imagine how it was ever possible for us to repose any weight on them. But there is no view of human life or of the condition of mankind, from which, without the greatest violence, we can infer the moral attributes or learn that infinite benevolence, conjoined with infinite power and infinite wisdom, which we must discover by the eyes of faith alone.[14]

In both of the above quotations, Kant and Hume seem to be saying that there is evidence for design, but that at most this shows that there might be a finite God, not the infinite, all-powerful God of classical theism. And of course, all of this fits right into Paulsen's thesis. Hume, Kant, and Mill, each of whom is skeptical of any rational theistic apologetic, do seem to admit that there is some support for the kind of God in whom Paulsen and the Mormons believe.

After quoting Kant and Hume, Paulsen goes on to outline his own teleological argument for Mormon theism. He does not go into great detail outlining the data ordinarily used to support the thesis that there is intelligent and purposeful design in the universe. Rather, he argues that finitistic, and especially Mormon, theism fits better with evidence for design (if there is evidence for design at all), and is therefore a better alternative than classical theism. Defining teleologically-ordered systems as systems exhibiting adaption of means to ends, Paulsen outline's his argument in the following way:

> 1. The universe is a member of the class of teleologically-ordered systems.
> 2. All members of this class whose origin we know (watches, houses, ships, etc.) are the products of intelligent design.
> 3. Hence, probably, the universe is of intelligent design.
> 4. Therefore, there is probably an intelligent designer of the universe whose natural faculties (intelligence, volition, power, etc.) are similar to, but far exceed, that of men.[15]

This argument, Paulsen admits, is basically one that is given by Cleanthes in Hume's *Dialogues Concerning Natural Religion*. Paulsen then cites a passage from Alvin Plantinga's analysis of Hume's argument. Plantinga presents some of the beliefs held by classical theists:

> (a) The universe is designed.
> (b) The universe is designed by exactly one person.
> (c) The universe was created *ex nihilo*.
> (d) The universe was created by the person who designed it.
> (e) The creator of the universe is omniscient, omnipotent, and perfectly good.
> (f) The creator of the universe is an eternal spirit, without body, and in no way dependent upon physical objects.[16]

Plantinga's conclusion is that though there might be a "smidgen" of evidence from the design argument for statement (a), the argument gives absolutely no support for statements (b)-(f). Paulsen goes on to comment that Plantinga underestimates the situation, for Paulsen thinks that the total evidence from the design argument works *against* propositions (b)-(f) being true, while at the same time providing support for finitistic theism. Paulsen lists six propositions of his own, which he believes are entailed by Mormon theism and fit better with the evidence of design.

(1_m) The earth and those portions of the universe on which human life depend are designed (ordered by intelligence).

(2_m) The earth, etc., may have been designed by a plurality of persons.

(3_m) The earth, etc., was organized out of pre-existing materials.

(4_m) The earth, etc., was organized by a plurality of persons.

(5_m) The principal designer and the principal organizer of the earth are omniscient, perfectly good, very powerful, but not omnipotent$_c$. [The subscript "c" stands for the type of omnipotence we ascribe to the God of classical theism in chapter 1.]

(6_m) The principal creators (i.e., designers-organizers) of the earth, etc., are eternal, materially embodied spirits which have materially necessary existence.[17] [The subscript "m" after each of the numbers stands for the Mormon series of propositions.]

Therefore, relying heavily on Hume's critique of the teleological argument, Paulsen concludes that the evidence from analogy leads to finite theism. This is because the Mormon theist does not assert that the entire universe was created out of nothing by an infinite God, but rather that only this earth was organized by beings who resemble us much more closely than does the God of classical theism. Says Paulsen:

(i) Any evidence of unorderedness or disorderedness in the universe would cohere with (rather than contra-indicate) Mormon theism.

(ii) The evidence which would count against a designer of the entire physical universe would count for (cohere with) Mormon theism.

(iii) Evidence of pre-existing materials being organized by a divine architect... would count for rather than contra-indicate Mormon theism.[18]

Pointing out that a complicated object that is being constructed is usually designed and built by more than one person, Paulsen contends that this analogy fits in better with Mormon rather than classical theism. Using analogy again, Paulsen also points out that since human builders use pre-existing materials, Mormon theism fits more closely with human design, for unlike the God of classical theism, the Mormon God used pre-existing material.

Paulsen also argues that Mormon (finitistic) theism better accounts for the facts of evolution. He writes:

> God's power must, hence, be understood not as power to abnegate such [physical] laws, but rather the power, based on His perfect and complete understanding of such laws, to maximally utilize these laws in the fulfillment of His purposes.... Accordingly, it is not necessarily inconsistent with Mormon theology to assert that God did (and had to) develop and perfect *mortal* life-forms by means of an evolutionary process, which, of necessity, required a long time period and the possibility of waste.[19]

In other words, since God is subject to certain eternal laws outside himself and must work in accord with these laws in order to accomplish his purposes, it is perfectly consistent with Mormon thought that God create life-forms by means of the natural laws which undergird the evolutionary process.

In summing up the arguments of the finitistic philosophers, we can conclude that there is a strong resemblance between the three positions we have covered. One point that they all have in common is that they believe that there is evidence of intelligent design in the universe. They also think that there is much disorder and evil in the world. Taking this position to its seemingly logical conclusion, they come to the position that the universe was designed, but by a being who was not all-powerful and had factors not totally under his control with which to contend. For Mill this was Matter and Force. For Brightman, it was the Given. For Paulsen and the Mormons, it is the uncreated and indestructible physical universe. That is, when creating, the creator had restraint placed upon him. The idea of an all-good omnipotent being seems to these thinkers impossible because of the reality of evil, and also because of the argument that an omnipotent being would not have to use a means to achieve his end (for a response to this, see Morris' comments in note 5).

Paulsen and the Mormons go a step further than the others, although they are perhaps merely taking finitistic theism to its logical conclusion. They say, based on the analogy from human affairs (from which most design arguments start), the concept of the Mormon God fits the data best. That is, since human beings are finite, embodied, and usually work in groups when building something, the Mormons and Paulsen say that it is reasonable to infer that the designers of the world are most likely similar. Thus, they find that Mormon theism, although based on alleged revelation, is the most logical and coherent theism one can support by appealing to the universe's apparent design. Therefore, Paulsen claims that Mormon theism seems to be the logical end result of a process in philosophy that has had several important names attached to it: the movement to a finite God.

A CRITIQUE OF THE MORMON USE OF THE ARGUMENT FROM DESIGN

Does the argument from design *really* support the idea of a finite God, and in particular, the finite God of Mormonism? Although there are a number of very highly respected names in support of this thesis—Hume, Kant, and Mill, among others—it seems that their position contains a fatal flaw: They explain the contingent order in the universe by appealing to a deity who is himself ordered and contingent. Thus, finitistic theism ultimately leaves unsolved the problem of how the order and design in the universe are to be explained. We will examine this flaw from two angles: (1) The idea of God as necessary being, and (2) The idea of a finite God as teleological explanation. We will conclude with (3) Other problems with the Mormon use of teleology.

The Idea of God as Necessary Being

In the first two chapters of this book, where we gave general descriptions of both the classical (chapter 1) and Mormon (chapter 2) concepts of God, we spent some time on the attribute of necessity. The conclusion we came to is that only the God of classical theism has real transworld necessity. Only the God of classical theism exists, if it is possible for Him to exist at all, in all possible worlds because He is the maximally greatest being. We made no attempt to try and show that He does exist, although both authors believe that there are convincing arguments for this God's existence.[20] Rather, we just tried to draw out some logical implications from what the classical theists have believed about God.

The finite God of Mormonism (and for that matter, the God of Mill and the God of Brightman) does not have this kind of logical or transworld necessity. He may have factual or material necessity in some worlds, i.e. (he may be uncaused or indestructible in some worlds), but he does not exist and possess these attributes in all possible worlds. But the question arises: Of all the possible worlds that could exist, why is this the one that does exist? Either this world was created by a logically necessary being, or it was not. These are the two exhaustive and exclusive possibilities.[21]

The first possibility is that this world exists because it was created by a logically necessary being. Since, by definition, He is the only being that exists in all possible worlds if He exists at all, only He is "behind" or "in back" of all possible worlds, and can choose which one will be actualized. Again, we are not trying to argue for the existence of such a God. We are just pointing out that if there is any concrete being (as opposed to an abstract being like the number 2) that exists in all possible worlds, it is He. Therefore, He would be the only being that would have, because of His transworld necessity and also His omnipotence and omniscience, the choice of which possible world is to really exist.

The other possibility is that there is no being that exists in all possible worlds; that the God of classical theism cannot possibly exist, since He must exist, if He does exist, in every possible world. The upshot of this possibility is that there is no reason why this world exists rather than another. There is no being to cause this world to exist, since there is no being that has transworld existence and necessity. Since there is therefore no rational being that stands "in back" of all possible worlds to choose to cause this world to exist, the reason that this one exists rather than another is therefore, ultimately, a matter of chance. Or to put it another way, since there are all sorts of possible worlds, and there is nothing that stands "behind" the possible worlds to be the reason for the existence of any one of them, the reason that this one exists instead of another is purely a matter of chance.

Keep in mind that the Mormon God is postulated as a teleological explanation for *this* earth, *not* the entire universe. For Mormon theism asserts that the universe as a whole has always existed and is in need of no ultimate explanation. Therefore, if the classical God does not exist, it is unnecessary to postulate the Mormon God as a teleological explanation for this world, since the universe as a whole exists by chance and is in need of no explanation. Why should worlds need explanations if universes don't? But if the classical God does exist, then there is no need to postulate the Mormon God to explain this particular world, since the being who exists in every possible world is the explanation for the entire universe including this world.

We believe that there are four possible responses to this line of argumentation. Let us critically examine each one.

1. THERE ARE NO POSSIBLE WORLDS. In order to undermine the concept of a being who exists in every possible world some deny that there are any other possible worlds. But this does not seem very plausible. For such a proposal would imply that this world is logically necessary, which seems absurd. For we can easily think of possible worlds which are different than this one and yet do not contain any logical impossibilities. But all such other worlds must necessarily be logically *im*possibilities if this is the only possible world, that any other world is logically impossible. But to say that our computer keyboard may be a different color does not seem logically impossible. That the South won the Civil War, although false, does not seem to have been logically impossible. Even that the laws of the universe be different than what they are now does not seem logically impossible, although it is *factually* impossible. For example, the speed of light is 186,000 miles per second, and cannot be any other speed in our universe. We doubt that it will change. For it to be 286,000 mps is factually impossible, but not logically impossible. It seems easy to believe that there are possible worlds where the speed of light is 286,000 mps. There does not seem to be a logical contradiction entailed by this possibility.

Furthermore, the Mormon cannot deny that there are other logically possible worlds, since to do so would be tantamount to saying that all creaturely actions could not have been otherwise. But such an admission would run in direct contradiction with Mormon metaphysics, which teaches both a strong libertarian view of freedom[22] and the doctrine that God became God because of his free choices (i.e., in some possible world God is not God).[23] Therefore, it seems obvious that there are other logically possible worlds.

2. IT MAKES NO SENSE TO ASK FOR A CAUSE FOR THE WHOLE UNIVERSE. The second objection goes something like this: it is illegitimate to ask about the cause of the universe, for Cause is a category that can only be applied to things which are within the universe. It is usually argued that the universe is eternal, and whatever is eternal does not need an explanation. Something quite close to this line of reasoning was presented by philosopher Paul Edwards in his paper "The Cosmological Argument." To quote Edwards:

> The demand to find the cause of the series as a whole rests on the erroneous assumption that the series is something over and above the members of which it is composed. It is tempting to suppose this at least by implication, because the word "series" is a noun like "dog" or "man." Like the expression "this dog" or "this man" the phrase "this series" is easily taken to designate an individual object. But reflection

shows this to be an error. If we have explained the individual members there is nothing additional to be explained. Suppose I see a group of five Eskimos standing on the corner of Sixth Avenue and 50th Street and I wish to explain why the group came to New York. Investigation reveals the following stories:

Eskimo No. 1 did not enjoy the extreme cold in the polar region and decided to move to a warmer climate.
No. 2 is the husband of No. 1. He loves her dearly and does not wish to live without her.
No. 3 is the son of Eskimos 1 and 2. He is too small and too weak to oppose his parents.
No. 4 saw an advertisement in the *New York Times* for an Eskimo to appear on television.
No. 5 is a private detective engaged by the Pinkerton Agency to keep an eye on Eskimo No. 4.

Let us assume that we have now explained in the case of the five Eskimos why he or she is in New York. Somebody then asks: "All right, but what about the group as a whole: why is it in New York?" This plainly would be an absurd question. There is no group over and above the five members, and if we have explained why each of the five members is in New York we have *ipso facto* explained why the group is there. It is just as absurd to ask for the cause of the series as a whole as distinct from asking for the cause of the individual members.[24]

This statement is paralleled by the one made by Bertrand Russell in his famous debate with Frederick Copleston. Russell stated, "The whole concept of cause is one derived from our observation of particular things; I see no reason whatsoever to suppose that the total has any cause whatsoever."[25] The whole line of argument that is taken here is that it is wrong to ask questions about the cause of the universe as a whole. For example, in the case of the Mormons, we could ask why any particular earth or God existed, but to ask why the Mormon universe as a whole existed, would be a meaningless question. According to this view, we can ask questions of cause and reason *within* the universe, not about the universe as a whole. But this whole approach seems to us to be flawed. William Rowe writes:

The principle underlying the Hume-Edwards criticism seems plausible enough when restricted to finite sets, i.e., sets with a finite number of members. But the principle is false, I believe, when extended to infinite sets in which the explanation of each member's existence is found in the causal efficacy of some other member. Consider M, the set of men. Suppose M consists of an infinite number of members, each member owing its explanation to some other member which generated it. Suppose further that to explain

the existence of a given man it is sufficient to note that he was begot-
ten by some other man. That is, where x and y are men and x begat y
we allow that the existence of y is explained by the causal efficacy of
x. On these suppositions it is clear that the antecedent of the principle is satisfied with respect to M. For every member of M has an
explanation of its existence. But does it follow that the existence of M
has an explanation? I think not. We do not have an explanation of M
until we have an explanation of why M has the members it has rather
than none at all. But clearly *all* we know is that there always have
been men and that every man's existence is explained by the causal
efficacy of some other man; we do not know *why* there always have
been men rather than none at all. If I ask why M has the members it
does rather than none, it is no answer to say that M always had
members.... To make this clear, we may rephrase our question as
follows: "Why is it that M has now and always had members rather
than never having members at all?" Surely we have not learned the
answer to this when we have learned that there always have been
members of M and that each member's existence is explained by the
causal efficacy of some other member.[26]

So it seems that the question of why this possible world exists rather
than some other possible world is a question that makes sense. And if it
makes sense to ask why this particular world exists, then it makes sense to
say that the universe as a whole is contingent and not necessary. For what is
necessary *must* be. So the point of all this is that the existence of any universe, if the God of classical theism does not exist, is uncaused and need not
have been. Hence, in answer to the question as to why the universe exists,
the Mormon theist must assert: There is no reason.

Richard Purtill points that if "we accept the No Reason view, that the
existence and nature of the universe are in need of explanation but cannot
be explained, it would be hard to see how we could have much confidence in
science." He concludes that "if there is no reason why the ultimate facts
about the universe are as they are, then there is no reason why they should
remain as they are and no reason why our apparent understanding of them
should not be completely illusory."[27] Hence, to say that the universe has no
reason for its existence is to resort to a form of skepticism, which under-
mines our confidence in both science and the ability of our minds to know
the world.

But the Mormons are likely to try to avoid this skepticism by defending what Purtill calls the Universe Ultimate view, a view which asserts that
the universe itself is the necessary being and that "the apparent order and
rationality of the universe are natural to it; the universe is by nature the sort
of universe which forms understandable patterns."[28] There are at least two
problems with this strategy. First, as Purtill points out:

If, as the Universe Ultimate view states, there is no intelligent power behind the universe, then everything in the universe is the result of the nature of the universe itself. That includes our own minds and their thinking about the universe. But if the universe is purely material and has no intelligent purpose, then our minds are the result of something that is without intelligence or purpose. However, if this is true, then what confidence can we have in the working of our minds? How can what does not have intelligence—a purely material universe—be expected to produce intelligence? Would we trust a computer somehow programmed by natural forces without intelligence?[29]

Although it is true that the Mormon view postulates eternally existent intelligences, the problem still arises as to *why* these intelligences exist at all, since these intelligences are not logically necessary beings (i.e., there are some possible worlds in which they do not exist). And even if the Mormon simply replies that these intelligences *just happen* to have always existed, then there is still no guarantee that our minds, which were at one time intelligences, can truly know the world, since the universe as a whole has no purposeful mind or intelligence to ground it. That is to say, if these intelligences *just happen* to exist, then there is no intelligent or purposeful ground to their existence). To put it another way, there are non-intelligent eternally existent entities in the Mormon scheme of things (i.e., matter/energy, moral laws, etc.) with which our minds interact and without which our minds would cease to exist (i.e., if the space/time matrix did not exist, then the intelligences would not exist; and if there were no eternal impersonal laws, both natural and moral, then eternal progression could not happen). Therefore, these non-intelligent entities, like the intelligences, are not logically necessary entities (i.e, there are possible worlds in which they do not exist). Hence, if there is no intelligent or purposeful ground to the universe as a whole, then our interaction with these non-intelligent entities is the result of something without purpose or intelligence, and thus there is no guarantee that our minds give us accurate information about the world and there is no reason why this particular universe exists rather than another.

Another problem with the universe-as-necessary-being view is that it seems to support classical theism. For instance, suppose that the Mormon argues that although particular objects in the universe—such as gods, worlds, cars, television programs, etc.—are different or non-existent in assorted possible worlds, the universe in its *essence* is necessary and hence exists in every possible world. However, a question immediately arises, "If the particular changing objects of the universe did not exist, would the necessary *essence* of the universe exist?" If the answer is "no," then the universe is not the necessary being for two reasons. First, a necessary being is *independent* and *self-sufficient* and hence would not need the particular changing objects of the universe in order to keep it in existence. Second, a necessary being who could cease to exist if other things ceased to exist would not exist in every possible world, since it would not exist in the world in which the particular changing objects of the universe did not exist, which the "no" answer clearly asserts. If the answer to our question is "yes," then the Mormon theist is admitting that there exists a being who exists independently of the changing universe and in every possible world. But this is the God of classical theism. Therefore, any attempt to say that the universe is the necessary being seems to support classical theism *not* Mormon theism.

3. A FINITE LOGICALLY NECESSARY BEING CAN EXIST. The third possible objection to our view is the one raised by Charles Hartshorne. This objection is that a finite being can be a logically necessary being and exist in all worlds, and therefore be the cause of the world. We have not discussed Hartshorne before, because, although a finitistic theist, he does not use the teleological argument. But his challenge to our critique of finitism cannot be ignored.

Hartshorne is a process theologian. The position that he defends is that God is finite but also logically necessary. If this is true, then it disproves what we have been saying about logical necessity and the God of classical theism.

Hartshorne was one of the first in this century to defend an ontological argument. He thinks that it does show the existence of a logically necessary being. God, for Hartshorne, exists in every possible world. But he is not the God of classical theism. Hartshorne is a panentheist, which is a compromise between theism and pantheism. Norman Geisler says this about Hartshorne's model of God:

> There is an actual pole and a potential pole in God. The potential pole is the order of all that can be, and the actual pole is the order of all that is. The former is God's "mind," and the latter is His "body." That is, the potential pole is God's conceptual vision and the actual pole is the physical realization of that vision. And since the actual world is in constant process, this pole is perishable; whereas the potential pole is imperishable. The potential pole is both absolute and eternal, but the actual pole is relative and temporal. What is more, the primordial (potential) pole is infinite (that is, indefinite) whereas the consequent (actual) pole is finite. So then God is actually finite but potentially infinite. He comprises the pole of changeless possibility and the pole of changing actuality.[30]

In short, God for Hartshorne has as his "mind" the ideas of what he could possibly be, while he has for his "body" the actual universe. Thus for Hartshorne, God's potential pole is the logically necessary being and the same in all worlds. But the actual pole is different in every world. God for Hartshorne is the greatest conceivable being. To quote Geisler again, "For Hartshorne, the world is based in God as the logically necessary ground of all contingency.... Hartshorne's God is the universal ground of all possible worlds."[31]

Although God for Hartshorne is not fully realized, He is ceaselessly striving to fulfill His potential and thereby endlessly surpassing Himself. Although God is always surpassing Himself, no other being can surpass Him. As Hartshorne says,

> God, however, is not simply more himself than any other can ever be; he and he alone is in all respects superior to any state that will ever characterize any individual unless it characterizes him. He is the greatest conceivable actuality, except perhaps as he himself can be conceived as greater.[32]

Is Hartshorne right? We do not think so. To quote Royce Gordon Gruenler (himself a former process theologian):

> ...[N]either in Whitehead's system nor in Hartshorne's has God any conscious personality over and above the world. His factual intent and consciousness are only in terms of this world. Hence He is "relatively" (R) dependent on us.... [I]n Hartshorne's system God is greater than the sum of the parts of the universe only in an abstract sense. Since we comprise his "brain cells," so to speak (Hartshorne's image), it is mystifying to comprehend in what substantial sense God is person apart from the world and can function as its chief lure for creative advance.[33]

In short, God as a maximally great being, and as a logically necessary being, is only the potential of what He could be. This is the same in every world. This hardly seems adequate. God, according to Hartshorne, is the potential pole (possibility) and the actual pole (the universe). This really does not seem to be saying more than there exists both a physical universe and ideals of what an absolute God would be like. For the ideal of what God as absolute could be could "exist" even in a world where there was no physical universe. But a mere idea of what God could be, is not the maximally great "being." And the actual pole can be surpassed by other beings in other worlds. Thus God, as an actual existing being, does not exist in all worlds and hence is not logically necessary. An ideal or possibility is not an actual being. For Hartshorne, chance, not God, is ultimate. "Literally all things, in their concrete details, happen by chance."[34] For Hartshorne God as actual being is a creature of chance and God as logically necessary is a mere abstraction, not a real being.

Indeed it appears that no finite being can be logically necessary. Recalling the God of classical theism, He is logically necessary because He exists in all worlds (and for other reasons, such as being infinite). Now a finite being, God or otherwise, cannot be a maximally great being, because being finite, no matter how great He is, it is logically possible that something greater could be.

If it is possible for the God of classical theism to exist in any world, He must exist in all worlds. He exists of His own necessity. Being the maximally greatest being who is infinite nothing else can cause or prevent His existence. But for a finite being, to be logically necessary He too would have to be both uncaused and the maximally greatest being. But if he were, then he would not be finite, since being finite, it is logically possible that any number of far greater and more powerful beings exist than He. This being the case, it seems impossible that He could be uncaused and/or the maximally greatest, because any number of superior beings that could cause or destroy Him can logically exist.

Moreover, since the God of classical theism exists (if He exists at all) of His own necessity, He cannot be changed by anything outside Himself. If He could be caused to be other than He is (if He is), He would not be necessary. But a finite being can be greater, or less, or qualitatively different. It does not seem that for a being of any given power, for example, that it is logically impossible that it has a different amount of power. It may be factually impossible, but not logically. But this being the case, no finite being can be necessary. For these reasons, it seems that a finite necessary being is impossible. At the least, if someone asserts that a logically necessary finite being is possible, the burden of proof is on him.

4. A LOGICALLY NECESSARY BEING IS IMPOSSIBLE. A fourth objection to our reasoning has its origin in the writings of David Hume.[35] Someone may agree with us that a logically necessary finite being is impossible and that because Mormon theism has no logically necessary ground for its universe, the universe exists for no reason whatsoever. But this person may go on to argue that this is no liability for Mormon theism, since the concept of a *logically necessary being* is incoherent, since (1) propositions about existence cannot be logically necessary and (2) the non-existence of a logically necessary being is conceivable.

The latter objection is contrasting the term "necessary being" with other logically necessary statements, such as

(a) All bachelors are unmarried males

and arguing that since a bachelor who is married is inconceivable, a necessary being who does not exist should also be inconceivable. But, it is argued, we can conceive of a necessary being as not existing, for people conceive of such a being not existing all the time (e.g., Mormons, atheists, agnostics, some theists, etc.). Hence, it is incoherent to speak of a "logically" necessary being.

Despite its initial plausibility, this objection seems fundamentally misguided. As Ronald Nash points out,

> Just because I find a state of affairs conceivable, it does not follow that it is logically possible. I might, for example, find it conceivable that the square root of 60,616 is 244. While it might be conceivable, it turns out to be logically impossible. I conclude then that. . .[this] argument against the doctrine of a logically necessary being turns out to be worthless.[36]

In other words, it does not follow from the fact that something is *psychologically* that it is logically possible. For example, Mormons and non-theists who argue against the logical possibility of the classical concept of God, would not be satisfied with a theistic response which asserts that because many theists find their own concept "conceivable," therefore the classical concept of God is logically possible. Moreover, we believe that there are certain religious concepts, such as reincarnation and the Mormon concept of God, which we find logically incoherent, although there are surely millions of people who find these concepts psychologically conceivable.

The former objection is arguing that the concept of necessity is something exclusive to propositions, not to reality. Consider the following:

(b) All triangles have three sides
(c) There are two metal triangles in the bedroom

The first proposition, (b), is logically necessary. Since a triangle by definition has three sides, necessarily, all triangles have three sides, whether or not any triangles exist in this world. The second proposition, (c), is claiming that something exists in reality; it is not describing a relation between two concepts in the proposition, as is (b). Because there is no contradiction in thinking of the bedroom containing no metal triangles, (c) is not logically necessary. Therefore, it is argued, since existing things, such as metal triangles, can be thought to have been otherwise without entailing a logical contradiction (unlike logically necessary propositions), God, who is claimed to be an existing thing, cannot be logically necessary.

Like (2), this objection is also flawed. First, (c) is a contingent state of affairs whose non-existence even the defender of a logically necessary being would concede involves no logical contradiction. Now if the objector offers us

(c$_1$) A logically necessary being does not exist

and asserts that this proposition involves no contradiction, he simply begs the question. For the point under question is whether (c$_1$) is logically possible. After all, an epistemological anarchist could argue against the possibility of consistently affirming *any* supposed necessary propositions by dogmatically asserting that

(b$_1$) All triangles do not have three sides

involves no contradiction. But without further argument this would simply assume the anarchist's point, and hence, beg the question. If the objector resorts to equating conceivability with logical possibility by asserting that he can *conceive* of a logically necessary being as not existing, then we are back to the first objection, which we have already shown to be in error.

Second, this objection to a logically necessary being is self-refuting. For the person defending it is really arguing:

(d) Necessarily, one can make no logically necessary statements about existence.

Now either (d) is a statement about existence or it is not. If it is not, then it is describing nothing about the real world, and hence, it is possible that a logically necessary being can exist. If (d) is a statement about existence, it is necessarily true in every possible world, for if it isn't then it is possible that a logically necessary being can exist. But if (d) is necessarily true in every possible world, then it is not true that one can make no logically necessary statements about existence, for (d) is a logically necessary statement about existence. Hence, this objection does not seem strong enough to overturn the coherency of the concept of a logically necessary being. In sum, not one of the four criticisms of our argument from necessary being against the Mormon concept of God is successful.

The Idea of a Finite God as Teleological Explanation

The argument from design does not make an appeal to a merely causal explanation, but also to a teleological one. A causal explanation is an explanation that shows how a certain thing is related to its cause, but a teleological explanation of something shows how that thing is designed. The argument from design appeals to certain facts about the world that seem to show that there must have been intelligent design. These include such things as the fact that the earth is arranged so that living beings can operate and survive on it and that everything in the universe seems to be mutually inter- dependent. The defender of the design argument then argues that to explain such an arrangement fully, we must postulate the existence of an intelligent mind(s) behind the organization of the world. Thus one argues from the earth, or the arrangement of the human body, to God.

But the finitistic philosophers are arguing back to a being who is Himself contingent, who exists only in some of the possible worlds, and in short, who did not have to be. Now teleological arguments are invoked by their defenders to explain the existence of ordered, designed relationships here in the universe. The defenders of a teleological argument believe that we must have a teleological explanation, one that explains why things are purposeful, when a purely causal explanation, particularly in terms of mechanism, would not do. The finite theists explain the existence of appar- ent design here on earth by an appeal to God.

For now let us assume that there is evidence of design in the world. But what does this prove? Well, it certainly does *not prove* the existence of the God of Mormon theism. Consider the following. The Mormons defend the existence of a finite God who is not logically necessary, a God who exists in only some of the infinite number of possible worlds. And this finite God is supposed to be the teleological explanation for the existence of the or- dered system of the earth. Furthermore, the Mormon God must be a highly ordered and purposeful being. And it seems intuitively obvious that in some respects a cause must be at least as great as its effects. However, a counter- example to this claim could be offered. It could be said that if a man builds an atomic bomb and drops it on Detroit, neither the man nor the bomb is as great as the devastation it causes. We can reply to this by saying that neither the man nor the bomb is a sole cause of the destruction. There are in the atoms in the explosive parts of the bomb tremendous energies holding the atoms together. These energies, when released by a mind, are greater than the force holding together the buildings in Detroit. So the cause, mind plus atomic energy, is at least equal to the destruction it causes. At any rate, it is apparent that the Mormon use of the teleological argument implies the truth of the principle that a cause must be at least as great as its effects (i.e., If this principle is not true, what then is the rationale for postulating the Mormon God?).

It follows from this that a God who designs and creates something like the earth must be, as far as order and intelligence and power, at least as great as the order and intelligent design of the earth. And for the Mormon God, this seems to be the case. But the Mormon universe is even more ordered than its finite God. For in the Mormon universe, we must remember, there exists over an infinite amount of space and time a system of extreme complexity. There are the primal intelligences being organized into persons, the infinite number of Gods creating persons and earths, and the infinite number of earths where persons are undergoing an "evolutionary" experience that is moving them to Godhood. The Mormon Gods have *always* existed in some state or another (i.e., all existed in the pre-godhood states of intelligence, pre-existence, and mortality) in the eternally existing and highly complex universe just described. But there is absolutely no explanation, either teleological or causal, for the existence of this possible world rather than another. That is, there would be no reason why the Mormon universe would exist. We have already seen that if the God of classical theism does not exist, then there is no being who exists in all possible worlds. Since there is then nothing "in back" of all possible worlds to actualize one of them, the fact that one of them exists, this one in particular, is a matter of chance. In short, the Mormons posit a universe of infinite complexity, which exists for no reason at all.

That is to say, for there to be a universe where a God can evolve, there must exist laws and conditions such that it is possible for a highly ordered and intelligent being to evolve. But, based on Mormon metaphysics, this means that these conditions exist by chance, since there is no higher intelligence than a finite God in Mormon theism to arrange these eternal conditions so that lesser Gods could evolve.

In sum, we can draw the following conclusions about the use of the argument from design in Mormon apologetics. First, the Mormons say that one should posit the existence of God (or Gods) because a highly ordered system shows purposeful arrangement of the parts to facilitate life and because it is impossible or unlikely that such an arrangement could arise by chance. But by the exact same logic, one must now ask for an explanation for the existence of the finite God and the universe he occupies. If ordered systems and beings require the teleological explanation of intelligent design, then by the same logic by which designers of the earth are postulated, designers of the finite Gods and the universe must be postulated. If a God, who can create an earth, can evolve and continue to exist by nonintelligent, nonpurposeful means, why not a world? If the Mormons think that the existence of just the earth requires a designing mind as an explanation, then how much more does the existence of the whole highly ordered infinite universe in which they believe. If ordered states of affairs require a cause, then the Mormon universe requires a cause. If ordered states of affairs do not require a cause, then the teleological argument for the Mormon God collapses.

Second, if a finite God can exist by chance and for an infinite amount of time that is beginningless in a possible world that exists for no causal or teleological reason, why couldn't an ordered earth also exist under the same circumstances? If a God can evolve on his own, why can't a world? Hence, if the complex and ordered universe as a whole can exist with no explanation, a less complex earth certainly can. Therefore, based on Mormonism's own metaphysical logic, there is no necessity to postulate the Mormon God to explain the earth.

Third, if there is an explanation for the design of the universe it is the God of classical theism who, because He is necessary and exists in all possible worlds, needs no explanation, teleological and/or causal, outside of Himself. If the argument from design does not work, then it provides no support for a theism of any kind. But if it does work, if there really is evidence of intelligent design here in the universe, then the God it leads to is the infinite God of classical theism. For any other finite God which is posited to explain design is Himself in need of explanation. Hence, if the principle that design demands a designer is correct, only the God of classical theism, and not a mere architect of the world, results. So, either the Mormons accept that their universe requires a transcendent necessary creator (e.g., the classical God) *or* deny that the teleological argument works. They must accept one of these positions. In short, to support their theory the Mormons must not only not use the teleological argument, they must argue *against* it.

We are not claiming the above proves the existence of the God of classical theism. For one thing, we have not provided any support for the validity of any teleological argument. We have just been bringing out the logical implications of the argument from design. Hence, what we do claim is that if the argument from design is valid, then it will lead us eventually to the God of classical theism. As far as we can see, the Mormon attempt to use teleology to produce a superior concept of God fails completely.

Other Problems With the Mormon Use of Teleology

The above arguments by themselves show that the finitistic theists (Mormon or otherwise) are wrong in thinking that the argument from design helps their position. But there are additional reasons for thinking that the concept of the Mormon God and the teleological argument are incompatible.

First, Paulsen and some other Mormon philosophers claim that their version of theism comes more naturally from analogy than does classical theism. Which is to say, in the argument from design we are reasoning from the world to God in the same way we reason from a house to a human being. Paulsen claims that using this analogy, the Mormon God, being much more like human beings than the God of classical theism, is the superior hypothesis. He claims that if we are reasoning from a design resembling a human's design what we arrive at should be more like a human. The God of classical theism is incorporeal, all-good, infinite, omniscient, omnipotent, one, eternal, etc., while the Mormon Gods are corporeal, finite, good, powerful (but not all-powerful), everlasting, and plural. Therefore, claims Paulsen, Mormonism is a superior hypothesis.

But if we are going to carry analogy to its logical conclusion, the Mormons have stopped short of what is the real logical conclusion. We should, if the theory of strict analogy is correct, go further than they do. We should posit beings who are powerful and knowledgeable, but who are not all good, die, fight among themselves (which would explain much of the disorder on earth), and some of which are deranged in some way. To quote Wesley C. Salmon on Hume's *Dialogues Concerning Natural Religion*:

> Philo drives the point home in the fifth dialogue with cutting wit: Taking account of the magnitude of the machine, and the imperfections in its constructions [i.e., the "machine" of the world], for all we know the world may have been created by a juvenile deity who had not yet learned his trade, or a stupid deity who only copies and does not do that very well, or a committee of deities, or a superannuated senile deity who had lost his knack by the time he got around to making our world.[37]

If we take too close an analogy from humanity, it seems to be impossible not to incorporate human weaknesses too. If we say that God is like a human being, there is no logical reason to stop with His being finite but wise and all good. We might as well end up at last with the Gods of early mythology: capricious, emotional, and morally reprehensible beings. In terms of the logical implications of its application of the teleological argument, Mormonism leads back to rank polytheism.

The final point is the problem of evil and disorder. It may at once be admitted that the concept of the finite God is compatible, as far we can see, with the evils and imperfections of the world. The trouble is that these evils and imperfections are just as compatible with a good deal else. To quote Gordon H. Clark's comments on Brightman's finite theism:

> Brightman of course wants a belief in a finite good god; but why cannot his arguments conclude with equal logic in favor of a finite evil god? The empirical method is as satisfactory for one as for the other. This world, so far as empiricism describes its past and refrains from unempirical prophecies, is just the type of world that would result from the activity of a finite evil god who does his best to make things unpleasant, but, being of limited intelligence and power, has not quite succeeded. He is unconquered by difficulty, however, and as far as we can see into the future we may be sure that he will continue to do worse and worse. Given a baffling mixture of good and evil, it is no more logical to believe in a little god than a little devil.[38]

Thus, the finite God hypothesis is not the only possible way to explain the disorder and order of the world, since the facts could be explained equally as well by a number of different hypotheses, such as an infinite God who is uninterested in morality, a couple of warring Gods (one good and one evil), senile deities, juvenile deities, insane deities, etc., etc. In other words, the finite but wise and good God of Mormonism is just one of a whole group of equally possible hypotheses which one can infer from the premises of Paulsen's argument from design. Therefore, there seems to be no reason why we should choose the Mormon deity to other versions of deity, at least on the basis of the design argument or because of evil.

NOTES FOR CHAPTER FOUR

1. New York: Simon & Schuster, 1982.

2. John Stuart Mill, *Nature, The Utility of Religion, and Theism* (London: Longermans, Green and Co., 1923), p. 167.

3. *Ibid.*, pp. 171-172.

4. *Ibid.*, pp. 28-29.

5. Thomas V. Morris points out at least two problems with this argument: "First of all, efficiency is always relative to a goal or set of intentions. Before you can know whether a person is efficient in what she is doing, you must know what it is she intends to be doing, what goals and values are governing the activity she is engaged in. In order to be able to derive from the story of evolution the conclusion that if there is a God in charge of the world, he is grossly inefficient, one would have to know of all the relevant divine goals and values which would be operative in the creation and governance of a world such as ours. Otherwise, it could well be that given what God's intentions are, he has been perfectly efficient in his control over the universe.... [Second], what is the property of being efficient, anyway? An efficient person is a person who husbands his energy and time, achieving his goals with little energy and time as possible. Efficiency is a good property to have if one has limited power or limited time, or both. But apart from such limitations, it is not clear at all that efficiency is the sort of property it is better to have than to lack. On the Anselmian conception of God, he is both omnipotent and eternal, suffering limitations with respect to neither power nor time. So it looks as if there is no good reason to think that efficiency is the sort of property an Anselmian being would have to exemplify." (Thomas V. Morris, *The Logic of Incarnate* [Ithaca, NY: Cornell University Press, 1986], pp. 77-78).

6. Mill, *Nature.*, p. 153. For philosophical and scientific critiques of this view, see chapter 3 of this present work; Francis J. Beckwith, *David Hume's Argument Against Miracles: A Critical Analysis* (Lanham, MD: University Press of America, 1989), pp. 76-82; Francis J. Beckwith, "Are Creationists Philosophically and Scientifically Justified in Postulating God?: A Critical Analysis of Naturalistic Evolution," *Interchange* (Australia) 46 (1989): 52-61; William Lane Craig, *The Existence of God and the Beginning of the Universe* (San Bernardino, CA: Here's Life, 1979), pp. 37-72; J.P. Moreland, *Scaling the Secular City* (Grand Rapids, MI: Baker Book House, 1987), pp. 22-38; and Richard Purtill, *Thinking About Religion: A Philosophical Introduction to Religion* (Englewood Cliffs, NJ: Prentice-Hall, 1978), pp. 52-55.

7. David Lamont Paulsen, *The Comparative Coherency of Mormon (Finitistic) and Classical Theism* (Ann Arbor, MI: University Microfilms, 1975), p. 18.

8. *Ibid.*, p. 32.

9. *Ibid.*, p. 33.

10. Edgar Sheffield Brightman, *A Philosophy of Religion* (Englewood Cliffs, NJ: Prentice-Hall, 1940), p. 229.

11. *Ibid.*, pp. 317-318.

12. Paulsen, *Comparative Coherency*, p. 154.

13. Immanuel Kant, *Critique of Pure Reason*, trans. and intro. Norman Kemp Smith (New York: Modern Library, 1958), pp. 293-294.

14. David Hume, *Dialogues Concerning Natural Religion*, in *Hume Selections* ed. Charles W. Hendel, Jr. (New York: Charles Scribner's Sons, 1927), pp. 369-370.

15. Paulsen, *Comparative Coherency*, p. 157.

16. Alvin Plantinga, *God and Other Minds* (Ithaca, NY: Cornell University Press, 1967), p. 109.

17. Paulsen, *Comparative Coherency*, p. 159. We believe that the reason for Paulsen's reference to several creators is that the Mormon prophet Joseph Smith taught that a counsel of Gods created the world. See Joseph Smith, *History of the Church of Jesus Christ of Latter-day Saints*, 7 vols., intro. and notes B.H. Roberts (Salt Lake City: Deseret Book Company, 1978), 6: 308. (*HC* from now on).

18. Paulsen, *Comparative Coherency*, p. 161.

19. *Ibid.*, p. 167.

20. See Beckwith, *David Hume*, chapter 5; Beckwith, "Are Creationists Philosophically and Scientifically Justified in Postulating God?; and Stephen M. Parrish, "Necessary Being and the Theistic Arguments," Ph.D. dissertation, Wayne State University (1991).

21. Someone may object that these are not the only two possibilities. Someone may argue that there might be more than one logically necessary concrete being. Pages 96-98 of this book indirectly address this problem when dealing with the argument that there could exist a logically necessary *finite* being. For a detailed and thorough discussion of this objection, see Parrish, "Necessary Being," chapter 4.

22. See Sterling M. McMurrin, *The Theological Foundations of the Mormon Religion* (Salt Lake City: University of Utah Press, 1965), pp. 77-82.

23. See *DH*, 6: 305-308.

24. Paul Edwards, "The Cosmological Argument," in *The Cosmological Arguments*, ed. Donald R. Burrill (New York: Doubleday, 1967), pp. 113-114.

25. Bertrand Russell and F.C. Copleston, "A Debate on the Existence of God," in *The Existence of God*, ed. John Hick (New York: Macmillan, 1964), p. 175.

26. William L. Rowe, "Two Criticisms of the Cosmological Argument," in *Logical Analysis and Contemporary Theism*, ed. John Donnelly (New York: Fordham University Press, 1972), pp. 35-36.

27. Purtill, *Thinking*, p. 10.

28. *Ibid.*

29. *Ibid.*

30. Norman L. Geisler, "Process Theology," in *Tensions in Contemporary Theology*, eds. Stanley N. Gundry and Alan F. Johnson (Chicago: Moody Press, 1976), p. 251.

31. *Ibid.*, p. 255.

32. Charles Hartshorne, "Alternative Conceptions of God," in *Religious Belief and Philosophical Thought*, ed. William P. Alston (New York: Harcourt, Brace and World, 1963), p. 336.

33. Royce Gordon Gruenler, *The Inexhaustible God* (Grand Rapids, MI: Baker Book House, 1983), p. 17.

34. Charles Hartshorne, "Religion in Process-Philosophy," in *Religion in Philosophical and Cultural Perspective*, eds. J. Clayton Feaver and William Horosz (Princeton, NJ: D. Van Norstrand, 1967), p. 266.

35. Hume, *Dialogues*; and David Hume, *An Enquiry Concerning Human Understanding*, 3rd ed., text revised and notes P.H. Nidditch, intro. and analytic index L.A. Selby-Bigge (Oxford: Clarendon, 1975; reprinted from the 1777 edition). For a brief overview of Hume's theory of knowledge, which is the basis for the view outlined in this text, see Beckwith, *David Hume*, pp. 19-23.

36. Ronald H. Nash, *The Concept of God* (Grand Rapids, MI: Zondervan, 1983), p. 110.

37. Wesley C. Salmon, "Religion and Science: A New Look at Hume's Dialogues," *Philosophical Studies* 33 (1978): 153.

38. Gordon H. Clark, *A Christian View of Men and Things* (Grand Rapids, MI: Eerdmans, 1952; reprinted ed., Grand Rapids, MI: Baker Book House, 1981), p. 277.

5
A BIBLICAL CRITIQUE OF THE MORMON CONCEPT OF GOD

The Bible is one of the standard works of the LDS church, along with the *Book of Mormon, Pearl of Great Price*, and *Doctrine and Covenants*. As we have pointed out in chapters 1 and 2 the Mormon concept of God differs radically from the classical concept of God. Traditional Christians have always taught that the classical view is the concept of God presented in the Bible. The Mormons, however, argue that their concept of God is closer to the Biblical portrait, although there are some individual Mormons who admit that some aspects of their view lack solid Biblical support.[1] We believe that the chief reason why Mormons and traditional Christians have derived from the same text diametrically opposed views of God is because the Mormons begin their interpretation of the Bible with the assumption that Joseph Smith is God's prophet and that his teachings are correct. And since Smith's teachings include the Mormons' unique concept of God, Mormons tend to "find" their view in the Bible. But in the process of "finding" their view Mormons are forced to reinterpret and strip out of context the meaning of passages which really do not support their view. Hence, only by *presupposing* the truth of their position are the Mormons successful in "finding" their concept of God in the Bible. Clearly this is a case of circular reasoning. That is, while interpreting the Bible the Mormons posit their doctrine of God based on Joseph Smith's teachings, and then they go to the Bible to support Smith's doctrine of God (see chart 5.1).

In this chapter we intend to show why the Mormon view is not found in the Bible and that the Bible's portrait of God is much closer if not identical to the classical concept. We will deal with the following topics: (1) Some general rules of interpretation, (2) There is only one God, (3) God as incorporeal, (4) God as Creator and Sustainer of the universe, (5) God as omniscient, (6) God as immutable and eternal, (7) God as omnipotent, and (8) God as omnipresent. The purpose of this chapter is two-fold: (1) to show why the classical concept of God rather than the Mormon concept makes better sense of the biblical data; and in the process (2) show why the Mormon interpretation of the Bible is inadequate.

Chart 5.1

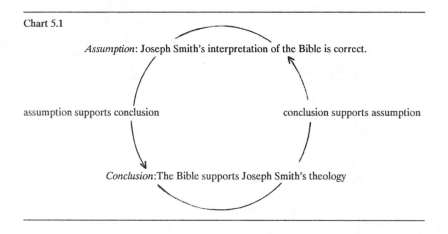

Assumption: Joseph Smith's interpretation of the Bible is correct.

assumption supports conclusion   conclusion supports assumption

Conclusion:The Bible supports Joseph Smith's theology

SOME GENERAL RULES OF INTERPRETATION

The science of interpretation is called *hermeneutics*. Over the centuries scholars have developed a number of rules for properly interpreting any piece of literature (in addition to the Bible). Although the question of how the Bible should be interpreted deserves book-length treatment,[2] a few basic guidelines should suffice for our present purposes. First, one should interpret the Bible as one would any ancient or modern text: permit the text to speak for itself. That is, unless the text is obviously symbolic or figurative because of clearly presented doctrinal beliefs within either the immediate context or other portions of Scripture, we should stick to the plain meaning of the text, and not read into the Bible doctrines that are otherwise totally foreign to text and can be textually justified *only* by *assuming* their truth.

Second, as Bruce Tucker points out, any Biblical passage should be interpreted in light of its "spheres of context" (see chart 5.2):

> Every word is part of a verse and every verse is part of a book. A verse is not independent from the verse around it. The authors of Scripture wrote sentence after sentence, never stopping to divide their work into chapters and verses. The verses are not a list of thousands of unrelated little ideas or profound magical truisms.
>
> Verses are often parts of a paragraph attempting to communicate a main idea. Sentences and clauses are grouped to explain, expand, or develop the main idea of the paragraph. Some sentence construction further explains the main idea of illustrating it or quoting other scriptural evidence. However, each sentence and verse is part of an uninterrupted context.
>
> When you attempt to understand a word, it is best defined by the words in its context. There are several spheres of context [such as similar types of writing, the Testament in which the verse is found, the entire Bible, and other contemporary writings], but the inner spheres [such as the phrase, clause, sentence, paragraph, book, and author's other writings] can most accurately give the meaning of the word or phrase in question.[3]

Chart 5.2[4]

Spheres of Context

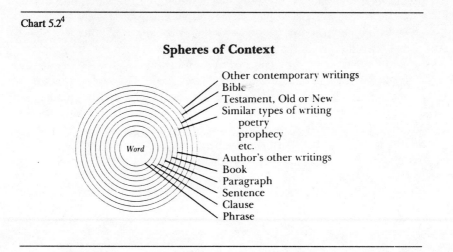

In other words, a passage of Scripture must be interpreted in light of both its immediate and general context. For example, it would be improper to interpret Joseph's relationship with the ruler of Egypt as similar to the one Andre Agassi has with John McEnroe (two professional tennis players) on the basis that the Bible teaches that Joseph "served in Pharaoh's court."[5]

Third, since our discussion focuses exclusively on the concept of God found in the Bible, it is important not to confuse passages that specifically speak of God's *essence* with those which describe God's *relationship* to humans.[6] For example, some passages in the Bible speak of God "repenting" (See Genesis 6:6; Exodus 32:14; 1 Samuel 15:11, 35), while other passages speak of God being unable to change his mind or "repent" (See Numbers 23:19; 1 Samuel 15:29). Some finite theists, such as the Mormons, cite the former passages as evidence against the classical view that God is immutable (that is, unchanging). But as Dr. Robert A. Morey points out, "none of the passages in question speak of a change in God's *nature*, but rather describe some *act* of God." And "all of these passages describe a change in God's works in terms of His revelation, relationship, or attitude toward man."[7] This is perfectly consistent with the classical concept of immutability outlined in chapter 1.

Fourth, it is incorrect to reason that because the Bible does not specifically forbid or mention something, therefore the Bible implicitly approves of it. People who reason this way are guilty of committing two logical fallacies: (1) argument from ignorance and (2) begging the question. The former occurs when one mistakenly argues that something for which one has no evidence is true because it has not been specifically disproved or denied. Begging the question occurs when one simply *assumes* what one is trying to prove, as in the case of the person who, when asked why he thinks the Celtics are the best team, answers, "Because no team is better." (begging the question is a form of circular reasoning, see chart 5.1). The following is an example of how these fallacies are committed in Biblical interpretation.

The Bible teaches in numerous places that only one God exists and that no other god will ever come into existence (e.g., Isaiah 43:10, 44:6-8). Some Mormons argue that the Bible is only talking about the God of this world, *not* the gods of the other worlds that exist in their universe. This, however, is strictly an argument from ignorance, for the Bible forthrightly asserts that no other god exists besides the one true and living God and it neither makes nor denies the god-of-this-world qualification. In other words, unless the Mormon *assumes* (that is, commits the fallacy of begging the question) her view to be correct prior to reading the text, a plain reading of the text does not support her view. This means that the classical theist has all the Biblical evidence in her favor, while the Mormon theist must commit the logical fallacies of begging the question and argument from ignorance in order to be correct.

THERE IS ONLY ONE GOD

As we just noted, Mormonism teaches that there exists more than one God. In fact, according to Mormon theology, an individual can progress to Godhood if he or she[8] obeys the appropriate precepts of Mormonism. In contrast, the Bible clearly teaches that there is only one Being Who by nature is God. Several passages clearly present this truth.

You yourselves are my witnesses—it is Yahweh who speaks—.... No god was formed before me, nor will be after me. (Isaiah 43:10)

Thus says Israel's king and his redeemer, Yahweh Sabaoth: I am the first and the last; there is no other god besides me. Who is like me? Let him stand up and speak, let him show himself and argue it out before me. Who from the very beginning foretold the future? Let them tell us what is yet to come. Have no fear, do not be afraid; have I told you and revealed it long ago? You are my witnesses, is there any other God besides me? There is no Rock; I know of none. (Isaiah 44:6-8)

Well then, about eating food sacrificed to idols: we know that idols do not really exist in the world and that there is no god but the One. And if there were things called gods, either in the sky or on the earth—where there certainly seem to be "gods" and "lords" in plenty—still for us there is one God, the Father, from whom all things come and for whom we exist; and there is one Lord, Jesus Christ, through whom all things come and through whom we exist. (I Corinthians 8:4-6)

For there is only one God, and there is only one mediator between God and mankind, himself a man, Christ Jesus. (I Timothy 2:5)

Other passages include Isaiah 45:5,18,21,22; Jeremiah 10:10; John 17:3; and I Thessalonians 1:9. Morey notes that there are many passages in the Bible which *seem* to teach the existence of many gods, but upon careful scrutiny one realizes that these passages are merely teaching that certain individuals have been looked upon by others as a god. Nowhere does the Bible teach that any other being is *by nature* a god except for the one true and living God.[9] Concerning these questionable passages, Morey writes:

...[T]he Bible uses the word "Elohim" (gods) in a figurative and symbolic way to refer to men and angels when they carry out a God-like function. Moses (Exodus 4:16) and the judges of Israel (Exodus 21:6; 22:8,9; Psalm 82:6) are called "gods" because, like God, they held the power of life and death over men.

...The figurative use of the word "gods" in the Bible should not be confused with polytheism, which is the belief in many gods. In John 10:30-36, when Jesus quoted Psalm 82:6 to the Jews who were about to stone Him, He was not saying that we should pray to or worship them. What he was doing was answering their objection to His claim of deity in verse 30. How could they get so mad at Him for claiming to be "God" when the word *Elohim* was at times even used of mere men such as the judges of Israel? He was greater than they because He was one in nature with the Father. The Jews got the point and picked up stones saying, "You being a man, make yourself out to be God." (John 10:33) They knew He was not just claiming to be "a god" in a figurative sense like the judges of Israel. He was claiming to be the one true GOD! This is why they screamed, "Blasphemy!"[10]

And nowhere in the Bible is the Mormon doctrine of eternal progression taught, that human beings can achieve godhood. As we noted above, any "successful" argument from the Bible to defend the Mormon view of polytheism must commit the logical fallacies of argument from ignorance and begging the question, and this is too high a price to pay for "biblical" support. Therefore, it is safe to say without reservation that the Bible supports strict monotheism, and hence, denies the existence of any god besides the one true and living God.[11]

GOD AS INCORPOREAL

Mormon theology teaches that God has a body of flesh and bones. But according to the Bible, God is *Spirit* in His essence and that which is spirit does not have a physical body, as the following passages indicate:

God *is* a Spirit: and they that worship him must worship *him* in spirit and in truth. (John 4:24—KJV)

Behold my hands and my feet, that it is I myself: handle me, and see; for *a spirit hath not flesh and bones*, as ye see me have. (Luke 24:39—KJV, emphasis ours)

This is why the Bible also teaches that God is not a man (Numbers 23:19) and why He is invisible (Colossians 1:15; 1 Timothy 1:17; Hebrews 11:27). Furthermore, if God is (1) omniscient, (2) omnipresent, and (3) creator and sustainer of all that is including both time and space (see a Biblical defense of these positions below), then it is *not* possible that God could be *essentially* corporeal.[12] For one reason, since corporeality presupposes the existence of time and space, and God would then be dependent on them for His corporeal existence, He cannot be their creator. Second, since a corporeal being is limited by time and space, its process of acquiring knowledge of events in the universe cannot exceed the limits of time and space (e.g., the speed of light). But since omniscience is at least the ability to know everything that is currently occurring and has previously occurred, God would have to exceed the limits of time and space to acquire this knowledge, for even if God's thought processes naturally exceed the speed of light (the fastest speed currently known to humans), they must have *some* speed. Hence, no matter how fast God's thoughts are, if He is limited by time and space, there would still be a period of time between an event occurring on the furthest edges of the universe and God knowing that the event has occurred. But if there was no such period of time, then He would know things *immediately*. But then He would in some sense transcend the limits of time and space and cease to be limited by them. Therefore, if God is essentially corporeal and hence limited by time and space, then for some period of time God would *not* be omniscient in the sense of knowing everything that is currently occurring or has occurred.

Furthermore, if God is omnipresent, as we believe the Bible clearly teaches (see below), he cannot by definition be limited by something which is spatio-temporal, such as a physical body. For obviously one cannot be present everywhere if one is located at some space and at some time, which logically follows from being corporeal. Consequently, if we can sufficiently demonstrate below that the Bible teaches that God is omniscient, omnipresent, and creator and sustainer of the universe, then we have further reason to believe that God is not corporeal.

The reader should take special notice of the fact of how the biblical attributes of God we just mentioned are interconnected: if God is omniscient, omnipresent, and creator and sustainer of the universe, then he must be incorporeal. And if he is incorporeal, the other three attributes are made possible. The interconnection of *all* the attributes will become apparent as we move along.

Prior to moving on, however, we do want to briefly respond to some popular Mormon objections to our conclusion. Mormons often argue that the Bible teaches that God has a body of flesh and bone by quoting such passages as Deuteronomy 34:10 ("Since then, never has there been such a prophet in Israel as Moses, the man Yahweh knew *face to face*." emphasis ours) and Exodus 33:21-23 ("And Yahweh said, 'Here is a place *beside me*.

You must stand on the rock, and when my glory passes by, I will put you in a cleft of the rock and shield you with *my hand* while I pass by. Then I will take *my hand* away and you shall see the *back of me*; but *my face* is not to be seen.'" emphasis ours). Several comments are in order.

First, the Mormon cannot use these passages, for they refer to the God of the Old Testament (Jehovah or Yahweh), a being who Mormons believe is the *pre-incarnate* Jesus,[13] a god *before* he became corporeal. Second, no passages in the Bible explicitly teach that God is by nature a corporeal being (that is, not one passage asserts "God has a body of flesh and bone"), although there are passages (see above) which teach that he is by nature Spirit. Third, it follows from this second point that the biblical passages that the Mormons cite to prove God's corporeality must be seen as either the use of physical language by the biblical authors to covey a particular meaning of God's actions in human terms or instances in which God temporarily assumes a physical form. This interpretation seems to make better sense of the Biblical text than the Mormon view. For if the Mormon view were taken to its logical conclusion then Mormons would have to admit that God possesses some very odd physical characteristics in addition to the human ones they are quite fond of. For example, the Bible teaches that the Holy Spirit manifested himself as a dove (Matthew 3:16), that God "covers you with his feathers, and you find shelter underneath his wings" (Psalm 91:4), that "our *God* is a *consuming fire*" (Hebrews 12:29; Deuteronomy 4:24), that God is a literal shepherd (Psalm 23), and that Jesus is a door (John 10:9), a loaf of bread (John 6:35,51), and a vine (John 15:1-5). Thus it is easy to see how ridiculous it is to interpret the nature of God in this way.

GOD AS CREATOR AND SUSTAINER OF THE UNIVERSE

As we noted in chapter 2 the Mormon God is *not* the creator of many entities in the universe, such as self-existent intelligences and the matter from which he "forms" the worlds he "creates." In contrast, classical theism teaches that there is nothing co-eternal with God. That is, the universe *began* to exist and God did *not* create it by using pre-existent matter, but merely created it out of nothing (in Latin, *ex nihilo*). The classical theist is not saying that the universe came from nothing, but that it was created by God from no other eternally existent substance. In this sense, the universe is absolutely dependent on God for its existence and therefore was created out of nothing. We believe that this view rather than the Mormon view best corresponds to what the Bible teaches. Our argument for believing that the Bible teaches creation *ex nihilo* is very simple:

> 1. The Bible *nowhere* teaches the Mormon doctrines of pre-existent matter and self-existent intelligences.
> 2. The Bible does teach that all that exists comes from God and is dependent on God for its existence.
> 3. The conjunction of 1 and 2 is identical with creation *ex nihilo*.
> 4. Therefore, the Bible teaches that God created the universe *ex nihilo*.

As far we know the first premise is rejected by no Biblical scholar, for the Bible *nowhere* teaches that the universe was created by God out of pre-existent matter or that there are self-existent intelligences that have always existed. Furthermore, the Bible nowhere teaches that anything is co-eternal with God, which would be necessarily true if the Mormon doctrine were the case. In fact, *only* God is referred to as a being who has always existed (e.g., Genesis 21:33; Exodus 3:15; Deuteronomy 33:27; I Chronicles 16:36; Job 36:26; Psalm 90:1-4, 102:12, 24-27, 145:13; Isaiah 40:28; Romans 1:20) Therefore, any Mormon attempt to "find" Biblical support for their doctrines is entirely question-begging.

Second, the Bible clearly teaches in numerous places that things other than God have not always existed. The following are a number of passages which clearly teach this doctrine.[14]

> Nor is he dependent on anything that human hands can do for him, since he can never be in need of anything; on the contrary, it is he who gives everything—including life and breath—to everyone. (Acts 17:25)

> [F]or in him were created all things in heaven and on earth; everything visible and everything invisible, Thrones, Dominations, Sovereignties, Powers—all things were created through him and for him. Before anything was created, he existed, and he holds all things in unity. (Colossians 1: 16,17)[15]

> All that exists comes from him; all is by him and for him. To him be the glory for ever! Amen. (Romans 11:36)

> It is by faith that we understand that the world was created by one word from God, so that no apparent cause can account for the things we can see. (Hebrews 11:3)[16]

It is the same God that said, "Let there be light shining out of darkness...." (2 Corinthians 4:6)

"You are our Lord and our God, you are worthy of glory and honor and power, because you made all the universe and it was only by your will that everything was made and exists." (Revelation 4:11)

From all of the above, a certain number of facts arise: (1) God has always existed; (2) the entities which make up the universe have not always existed; (3) God is the creator, sustainer, and *sole* cause of everything in the universe, which means there was no *material* cause of the universe; and (4) God created light out of darkness, which clearly implies something out of nothing. The only consistent theory to explain these facts is that God created the universe *ex nihilo*. Furthermore, since space and time are essential attributes of created things, and created things by definition occupy time and space, and God is not a created thing, God is the creator of time and space. For if God were limited by time and space, then they would not depend upon God for their existence (they would be just as eternal as God).[17] But, as we have seen, this clearly conflicts with the biblical view that God created *all* things. This has clear implications for our presentation of the remaining attributes of God we find in the Bible.

Against the doctrine of creation *ex nihilo*, Joseph Smith has argued:

> You ask the learned doctors why they say the world was made out of nothing, and they answer, "Doesn't the Bible say He *created* the world?" And they infer, from the word create, that it must have been made out of nothing. Now, the word created came from the word *baurau*, which does not mean to create out of nothing; it means to organize; the same as a man would organize materials and build a ship. Hence we infer that God had materials to organize the world out of chaos—chaotic matter, which is element, and in which dwells all the glory. Element had an existence from the time He had.[18]

Smith is right that the word *baurau* can be used to mean "to create something out of pre-existent materials," which would be consistent with the Mormon doctrine of creation.[19] However, there is no absolutely unambiguous indication in the passage which Smith is paraphrasing (Genesis 1:1) that *baurau* is being used in either the Mormon sense or in the classical sense of creation *ex nihilo*, although most scholars would argue it is being used in the latter sense.[20] In other words, the mere fact that a Biblical passage appears to be *consistent* with a Mormon doctrine does not mean that the Bible *as a whole* teaches that doctrine, or that the particular passage under question is really teaching that doctrine. For, as in this case, the word *baurau* is also consistent with the doctrine of creation *ex nihilo*, as present scholarship indicates.[21] This response is adequate to take care of other passages that a Mormon apologist may use, such as those which teach that God *formed*, *fashioned* or *made* particular things in the world (e.g., Genesis 2:7; Isaiah 45:7). Once again, although these passages are superficially consistent with the Mormon view, they are also consistent with creation *ex nihilo*. Therefore, given the entire testimony of Scripture (see above), the conclusion seems inescapable: the Bible teaches that God created the universe out of nothing.

GOD AS OMNISCIENT

In chapter 2 we pointed out that a number of Mormon scholars have taught that God does not have knowledge of the future, since He is limited by time and space and therefore only has knowledge of everything that *can* be known, namely, the past and the present.

We believe that the Mormon view clearly conflicts with the biblical presentation that God has complete knowledge of the past, present, and *future*.[22] God's knowledge is so vast that the Psalmist writes: "God, how hard it is to grasp your thoughts! How impossible to count them! I could no more count them than I could count sand, and suppose I could, you would still be with me." (139:17,18)   The Psalmist writes elsewhere that "our Lord is great, all-powerful, of infinite understanding." (147:5) Concerning God's knowledge the present, the author of Job writes of God, "For he sees to the ends of the earth, and observes all that lies under heaven" (28:24). Since what is the past was once the present, and God has total knowledge of the present, it follows that God has total knowledge of the past (see Isaiah 41:22). Concerning the future, Isaiah quotes God has saying, "From the beginning I foretold the future, and predicted beforehand what is to be. I say: My purpose shall last; I will do whatever I choose." (46:10) In another place Isaiah quotes Yahweh as saying that knowledge of the future is essential for deity:

> "Produce your defense," says Yahweh, "present your case," says Jacob's king. "Let them come forward and tell us what is going to happen next. What could they tell us of the past to make it worth our notice? Or will you discourse to us of future things and let us know their outcome? Tell us what is to happen in the future, and so convince us you are gods. Do something at least so that we can note it and all see it. No, you are nothing and your works are nothingness; to choose you would be an outrage." (41:21-24).

God's knowledge of the future is also asserted in the New Testament teaching that God foreknows who will be saved (see Romans 8:29 and I Peter 1:1-2). Although there are numerous other passages that imply and affirm God's knowledge of the future,[23] it is interesting to note that one can infer God's absolute knowledge of the future from His test of a true prophet in Deuteronomy 18:22:

> When a prophet speaks in the name of Yahweh and the thing does not happen and the word is not fulfilled, then it has not been spoken by Yahweh. The prophet has spoken with presumption. You have nothing to fear.

If, of course, God does not know the future and prophecy involves an extrapolation from current knowledge to a highly probable future event, as some Christian philosophers and theologians have claimed (e.g., Pinnock writes that some prophecies are "predictions based on God's exhaustive knowledge of the past and present."[24]), it is within the realm of possibility that God could make a mistake. But if it is both true that He can make a mistake and that Deuteronomy 18:22 is normative for prophet status, then it is possible that Yahweh can speak a prophecy which does not come to pass and at the same time we would be perfectly correct in saying that Yahweh had not spoken, although our judgment would be false. In other words, in some possible world Yahweh does not speak for Yahweh. Hence, only if God has absolute knowledge of the future does Deuteronomy 18:22 make sense.

GOD AS IMMUTABLE AND ETERNAL

As we pointed out in chapter 2, Mormonism teaches that God is mutable. For it is taught that there was a time when God did not exist as God, and some Mormons teach and have taught that God is increasing in both knowledge and power. This view clearly conflicts with the view of God presented in the Bible.

In Malachi (3:6) God is quoted as saying, "I, Yahweh, do not change...." The Scriptures teach that "God's counsels are not subject to change, fluctuation, or failure." According to Alan Gomes, "Biblically, the word 'counsel' refers to one's intention resolution, will, or purpose."[25] And this is why the Bible teaches that God's purposes are "unalterable" (Hebrews 6:17). God says in Isaiah (46:10b): "My purpose shall last; I will do whatever I choose." Furthermore, the Bible teaches that God has always been God, that He is an eternal being:

> Before the mountains were born, before the earth or the world came to birth, you were God from all eternity and for ever. (Psalm 90:2)

> Yahweh is an everlasting God, he created the boundaries of the earth. He does not grow tired or weary, his understanding is beyond fathoming. (Isaiah 40:28)

> ...I am your God, I am he from eternity. No one can deliver from my hand, I act and no one can reverse it. (Isaiah 43:12b,13)

> For thus speaks the Most High, whose home is in eternity, whose name is holy (Isaiah 57:15a)

> Ever since God created the world his everlasting power and deity—however invisible—have been there for the mind to see in the things he has made. (Romans 1:20a)

> To the eternal King, the undying, invisible and only God, be honor and glory for ever and ever. Amen. (I Timothy 1:17)

These are not the only passages which teach that God has always existed,[26] although they are sufficient for our current purposes. Now an important observation follows when one considers God's immutability and eternal nature along with the other Biblical attributes of God we have already covered (incorporeal, sustainer and creator of the universe, omniscient). If God is sustainer and creator of the universe (and hence unlimited by time and space), unchanging in his nature, and eternal, it follows that in some sense God is timeless. This does not mean that God does not act in time or that His acting in time is an assault upon His immutability, but simply that he is not bound by time and that His changing actions toward His creation are active and personal responses of His unchanging nature, which He knew from all eternity would occur. Since we have already covered some of the philosophical objections to immutability and timelessness elsewhere in this text, we refer the reader to that section of chapter 1.

GOD AS OMNIPOTENT

We noted in chapter 2 that the Mormon view of God denies that God is all-powerful in the sense that he cannot destroy matter and its laws. In order for God to act He must use the matter and laws that are at his disposal. The God of Biblical theism, however, is the creator of everything, including matter and its laws (see the appropriate section in this chapter). In light of this doctrine of creation, one can see that the Bible clearly teaches that God is limited by nothing external to Himself:[27]

I know that you are all-powerful: what you can conceive, you can perform. (Job 42:2)

Ah, Lord Yahweh, you have made the heavens and the earth with your great power and outstretched arm. To you nothing is impossible. (Jeremiah 32:17)

Jesus gazed at them, "For men," he told them, "this is impossible; for God everything is possible." (Matthew 19:26)

... for nothing is impossible to God. (Luke 1:37)

It bears repeating what we pointed out in chapter 1, namely, that God's omnipotence must be qualified by saying that God can do anything that is (1) logically possible and (2) consistent with him being a wholly perfect, personal, disembodied, omniscient, immutable, necessary creator. These attributes do not limit God in any *real* sense, but are *perfections*, attributes at their infinitely highest level which are essential to God's nature. To put it another way, since God is a perfect person, He cannot do anything that is in violation of his perfect character, but this hardly counts against His omnipotence, for how can acting in accordance with *perfection* be *limiting* (i.e., to be limited is to be *im*perfect)? This is consistent with the biblical portrayal of God being incapable of sinning (Mark 10:18, Hebrews 6:18), ceasing to exist (Exodus 3:14, Malachi 3:6), or not knowing something (Job 28:24, Psalm 139:17-18, Isaiah 46:10a). The first qualification—God can do only that which is logically possible—does not conflict with the Biblical assertion that *nothing* is impossible to God. For, as we noted in chapter 1, a logically impossible "entity," such as a square-circle, a married-bachelor, or a sighted invisible object, is not really a *thing*. It is merely a combination of contradictory terms which are strung together and appear to say *some thing*, but in fact refer to an "entity" which is not even a "something" which we can suppose to be true. For a logically impossible "entity" cannot be a possible "thing". Hence, it does not count against God's omnipotence that He cannot bring into existence that which is not even logically possible (see further explanation in chapter 1).

GOD AS OMNIPRESENT

Since the Mormon God has a physical body, and hence is limited by time and space, He cannot be present everywhere at once. For this reason, when the Mormon says that God is omnipresent, he is asserting that God's influence, power, and knowledge are all-pervasive, but that the focal point of God's being (that is, his body) exists at a particular place in time and space. We believe that this view of omnipresence differs radically from the view of omnipresence found in the Bible.

> Understand this today, therefore, and take it to heart: Yahweh is indeed, in heaven above as in earth beneath, he and no other. (Deuteronomy 4:39)

> Yet will God really live with men on the earth? Why, the heavens and their own heavens cannot contain you [God]. How much less this house that I have built. (I Kings 8:27)[28]
> The house I am building will be large, for our God is greater than all gods. Who would have the means to build him a house when the heavens and their own heavens cannot contain him? (2 Chronicles 2:5,6)

> Since the God who made the world and everything in it is himself Lord of heaven and earth, he does not make his home in shrines made by human hands. Nor is he dependent on anything that human hands can do for him, since he can never be in need of anything; on the contrary, it is he who gives everything—including life and breath—to everyone. From one single stock he not only created the whole human race so that they could occupy the entire earth, but he decreed how long each nation should flourish and what the boundaries of its territory should be. And he did this so that all nations might seek the deity and, by feeling their way toward him, succeed in finding him. Yet in fact *he is not far from any of us, since it is in him that we live, and move, and exist*, as indeed some of your own writers have said.... (Acts 17:24-28—emphasis ours)[29]

As we noted in chapter 1, it seems philosophically sound to assert that God's omnipresence logically follows from His omniscience, disembodiment, omnipotence, and role as sustainer and creator of the universe. It seems that the biblical writers arrived at the same conclusion. For if God knows everything immediately without benefit of sensory organs, is not limited by any particular spatio-temporal body, and sustains the existence of all dependent reality, it follows that God is in some sense present everywhere. Hence, as we pointed out earlier in this chapter, the classical attributes of God are interconnected and form a coherent picture which make much better sense of the data of Scripture than the attributes of the Mormon concept of God.

NOTES FOR CHAPTER FIVE

1. For example, Van Hale, Mormon publisher of the *Mormon Miscellaneous* reprint and pamphlet series, comments on the Mormon view of procreated pre-existence and confesses that "Mormons sometimes cite several New Testament passages in support" of this doctrine (e.g., Heb. 12:9, Acts 17:28, Galatians 4, and Romans 8), although "these passages do not state that God procreated our spirits...." For "the more likely intent of these biblical authors is that God is the father of those who accept the gospel and are adopted as his spiritual children." (Van Hale, "The Origin of the Human Spirit in Early Mormon Thought," in *Line Upon Line: Essays on Mormon Doctrine*, ed. Gary James Bergera [Salt Lake City, UT: Signature Books, 1989], p. 115).

2. See especially, Walter C. Kaiser, Jr., "Legitimate Hermeneutics," in *Inerrancy*, ed. Norman L. Geisler (Grand Rapids, MI: Zondervan, 1980), pp. 117-150; Bernard Ramm, *Protestant Biblical Interpretation*, rd rev. ed. (Grand Rapids, MI: Baker Book House, 1970); James Sire, *Scripture Twisting* (Downers Grove, IL: InterVarsity Press, 1980); and Bruce Tucker, *Twisting the Truth* (Minneapolis: Bethany House, 1987).

3. Tucker, *Twisting*, pp. 147-148.

4. Chart from *Ibid.*, p. 148.

5. Sire, *Scripture*, pp. 65-66.

6. For a brief overview of how a similar hermeneutical mistake occurs in the Christian doctrine of the Resurrection, see Francis J. Beckwith, "Identity and Resurrection: A Review Article," *Journal of the Evangelical Theological Society* 33 (September 1990): 369-373.

7. Robert A. Morey, *Battle of the Gods* (Southbridge, MA: Crown Publishing, 1989), p. 222.

8. According to Mormon theology, the God of earth has a wife-goddess to whose status Mormon women may aspire. See Linda P. Wilcox, "The Mormon Concept of a Mother in Heaven," in *Line Upon Line*, pp. 103-113.

9. Morey, *Battle*, pp. 182-183.

10. *Ibid.*

11. It should be noted that the traditional Christian doctrine of the Trinity is *monotheistic*, not *polytheistic*. For the doctrine of the Trinity asserts that three divine *persons* share the same substance or essence (i.e., the three persons are one and the same God). Since a biblical and philosophical defense of this doctrine falls outside the scope of this book, we suggest the following works: J. Kenneth Grider, "The Holy Trinity," in *Basic Christian Doctrines*, ed. Carl F.H. Henry (New York: Holt, Rinehart and Winston, 1962), pp. 35-41; C. Stephen Layman, "Tritheism and the Trinity," *Faith and Philosophy* 5 (July 1988): 291-298; Walter R. Martin, *Kingdom of the Cults*, rev. ed. (Minneapolis: Bethany House, 1977), pp. 53-84; Thomas V. Morris *The Logic of God Incarnate* (Ithaca, NY: Cornell University Press,

1986), pp. 205-218; Richard Swinburne, "Could There Be More Than One God," *Faith and Philosophy* 5 (July 1988): 225-241; Tucker, *Twisting*, pp. 59-93; and Ruth A. Tucker, *Another Gospel* (Grand Rapids, MI: Zondervan/Academie, 1989), pp. 399-403.

12. Although traditional Christians believe that Jesus of Nazareth was both corporeal and God the Son at the same time, they do *not* believe that *God the Son* is essentially corporeal. That is, God the Son acted in time and space but was not essentially limited by them. Therefore, the objections in the text to the Mormon God do not apply to Jesus of Nazareth who, although taking on a human nature, never relinquished his eternal timeless status as God the Son, a person not essentially limited by time and space. And since the Mormon God is essentially corporeal, there is no timeless and/or spaceless aspect to his nature. Since a complete philosophical defense of this view of the incarnation is outside the scope of this book, we refer the reader to Morris' *Logic*, pp. 56-107.

This is why David Paulsen is incorrect in his observation that since "natural theologians have argued that God (logically) must be incorporeal, without body or parts. . . [this] apparently contradicts the common Christian belief that God (the Son) was incarnate in the person of Jesus of Nazareth, and now exists everlastingly with a resurrected body." (David Paulsen, "Must God Be Incorporeal?" *Faith and Philosophy* 6 [January 1989]: 76). The problem with Paulsen's observation is that he doesn't seem to recognize the fact that these natural theologians also asserted that God the Son's corporeality is not essential to his nature; that is, if God had created another possible world in which redemption through incarnation was not necessary, God the Son would have never become incorporeal. Therefore, there is no contradiction in asserting that God is essentially incorporeal and that God the Son *took on* a human nature that is unessential to his status as God the Son.

13. Mormon theologian Bruce McConkie writes, "Christ is *Jehovah*; they are one and the same Person." (Bruce McConkie, *Mormon Doctrine*, 2nd ed. [Salt Lake City, UT: Bookcraft, 1979], p. 392). However, some Mormon scholars admit that it is not always clear in Mormon literature as to whom the title Jehovah refers. See Boyd Kirkland, "Elohim and Jehovah in Mormonism and the Bible," *Dialogue: A Journal of Mormon Thought* 19 (Spring 1986): 77-93; and Boyd Kirkland, " Jehovah as the Father," *Sunstone* 9 (Autumn 1984): 36-44.

14. For more passages that explicitly or implicitly teach this doctrine, see Augustus Hopkins Strong, *Systematic Theology: A Compendium* (Old Tappan, NJ: Fleming Revell, 1907), pp. 374-378.

15. One of the authors of this text has used these creation passages to produce a deductive argument that shows that the Bible teaches that Jesus is God. See Francis J. Beckwith, "Of Logic and Lordship: The Validity of a Categorical Syllogism Supporting Christ's Deity," *Journal of the Evangelical Theological Society* 29 (December 1986): 429-430.

16. Since pre-existent matter would be the *material* cause of the universe, and since this passage teaches that no cause except God can account for the universe, this passage clearly teaches creation *ex nihilo*.

17. This brief argument is derived from Morey, *Battle*, p. 203.

18. Joseph Smith, *History of the Church of Jesus Christ of Latter-Day Saints*, 7 vols., intro. and notes B.H. Roberts, 2nd ed. rev. (Salt Lake City: The Deseret Book Company, 1978), 6:308.

19. See *Nelson's Expository Dictionary of the Old Testament*, eds. Merrill F. Unger and William White, Jr. (Nashville: Thomas Nelson, 1980), p. 84.

20. See *Ibid*.

21. The contributors in *Ibid*. state that present scholarship not only holds that Genesis 1:1 is consistent with creation out of nothing, but in fact teaches it. But even if scholarship were evenly divided, this would be woefully insufficient to say the Bible actually *teaches* the Mormon doctrine of creation.

22. For greater detail and more Scripture references than what is presented here, see William Lane Craig, *The Only Wise God* (Grand Rapids, MI: Baker Book House, 1987), pp. 21-37; and Morey, *Battle*, pp. 229-241.
There are some Christian theists who hold a view concerning God's omniscience which is similar to the Mormon view outlined in this text, although we believe that their view, like the Mormon view, is unbiblical. For defenses of this position, see Clark Pinnock, "God Limits His Knowledge," in *Predestination and Free Will*, eds. David Basinger and Randall Basinger (Downers Grove, IL: InterVarsity Press, 1986), pp. 141-162; Richard Rice, "Divine Foreknowledge and Free-Will Theism," in *The Grace of God, The Will of Man*, ed. Clark H. Pinnock (Grand Rapids, MI: Academie/Zondervan, 1989), pp. 121-139; Richard Rice, *God's Foreknowledge and Man's Free Will* (Minneapolis: Bethany House, 1985); and Richard Swinburne, *The Coherence of Theism* (Oxford: Clarendon, 1977), pp. 167-178. For responses to this view and defenses of what we believe is the biblical view, see the responses by John Feinberg, Norman Geisler, and Bruce Reichenbach in *Predestination and Free Will*, pp. 163-177; Craig, *The Only Wise God*, pp. 39-44; Alan W. Gomes, "God in Man's Image: Foreknowledge, Freedom, and the 'Openness' of God," *Christian Research Journal* 10 (Summer 1987): 18-24; and Morey, *Battle*, pp. 229-241.

23. For more biblical passages, see Craig, *The Only Wise God*, pp. 25-37; and Morey, *Battle*, pp. 229-241.

24. Pinnock, "God Limits His Knowledge," p. 158. See also, Clark H. Pinnock, "From Augustine To Arminius: A Pilgrimage in Theology," in *The Grace of God*, pp. 25-26; and Clark H. Pinnock, "Between Classical and Process Theology," in *Process Theology*, ed. Ronald H. Nash (Grand Rapids, MI: Baker, 1987), p. 325.

25. Gomes, "God in Man's Image," p. 20.

26. For more passages, see Morey, *Battle*, pp. 203-208.

27. For more passages, see Morey, *Battle*, pp. 243-247.

28. This particular passage cannot be used against the doctrine of the incarnation —that God took on human nature in the person of Jesus of Nazareth—because the passage in question is simply stating that God cannot be contained by a finite reality (in this instance, a temple). In contrast, the doctrine of the incarnation entails that God *took on* a human nature

in addition to His divine nature, *not* that God's being was contained by human nature. Hence, the passage in question cannot be used against God becoming man in Jesus of Nazareth. For a philosophical defense of this view, see Morris, *Logic*.

29. For more passages, see Morey, *Battle*, pp. 225-227.

BIBLIOGRAPHY

BOOKS

Andrus, Hyrum L. *God, Man and the Universe*. Salt Lake City: Bookcraft, 1968.

Anselm. *Basic Writings*. Translated by S.N. Deane. 2nd edition. LaSalle, IL: Open Court, 1962.

Aquinas, Thomas. *An Aquinas Reader*. Edited and Introduction by Mary T. Clark. Garden City, NY: Image Books, 1972.

_____. *Introduction to Saint Thomas Aquinas*. Edited and Introduction by Anton C. Pegis. New York: The Modern Library, 1948.

Basinger, David and Basinger, Randall, eds. *Predestination and Free Will*. Downers Grove, IL: InterVarsity Press, 1986.

Beckwith, Francis J. *Baha'i*. Minneapolis: Bethany House, 1985.

_____. *David Hume's Argument Against Miracles: A Critical Analysis*. Lanham, MD: University Press of America, 1989.

Beckwith, Francis J. and Parrish, Stephen E. *See the Gods Fall*. Nashville: Thomas Nelson, 1992.

Bergera, Gary James, ed. *Line Upon Line: Essays on Mormon Doctrine*. Salt Lake City, UT: Signature Books, 1989.

Brightman, Edgar Sheffield. *A Philosophy of Religion*. Englewood Cliffs, NJ: Prentice-Hall, 1940.

Clark, Gordon H. *A Christian View of Men and Things*. Grand Rapids, MI: Eerdmans, 1952. Reprinted edition, Grand Rapids, MI: Baker Book House, 1981.

Clarke, W. Norris. *The Philosophical Approach to God*. Winston-Salem, NC: Wake Forest University Press, 1979.

Craig, William Lane. *The Cosmological Argument From Plato to Leibniz*. London: Harper & Row, 1980.

_____. *The Existence of God and the Beginning of the Universe*. San Bernardino, CA: Here's Life, 1979.

_____. *The Kalam Cosmological Argument*. New York: Barnes & Noble, 1979.

_____. *The Only Wise God*. Grand Rapids, MI: Baker Book House, 1987.

Fraenkel, Abraham. *Abstract Set Theory*. Amsterdam: North-Holland Publishing, 1961.

Fraser, Gordon H. *Sects of the Latter-day Saints*. Eugene, OR: Industrial Litho, 1978.

Geisler, Norman L. and Corduan, Winfried. *Philosophy of Religion*. 2nd edition. Grand Rapids, MI: Baker Book House, 1988.

Geisler, Norman L. and Watkins, William. *World Apart*. 2nd edition. Grand Rapids, MI: Baker Book House, 1989.

Gruenler, Royce Gordon. *The Inexhaustible God*. Grand Rapids, MI: Baker Book House, 1983.

Hoyle, Sir Frederick and N. Chandra Wickramasinghe. *Evolution From Space*. New York: Simon & Schuster, 1982.

Hume, David. *Dialogues Concerning Natural Religion*. Edited by Nelson Pike. Indianapolis: Bobbs-Merrill, 1970.

_____. *Enquiry Concerning Human Understanding*. 3rd edition. Text revised and Notes by P.H. Nidditch. Introduction and Analytic Index by L.A. Selby-Bigge. Oxford: Clarendon, 1975. Reprinted from the 1777 edition.

_____. *The Letters of David Hume*. Edited by J.Y.T. Greig. 2 volumes. Oxford: Clarendon, 1932.

Jastrow, Robert. *God and the Astronomers*. New York: Norton, 1978.

Kant, Immanuel. *Critique of Pure Reason*. Translated and Introduction by Norman Kemp Smith. New York: The Modern Library, 1958.

Mackie, J.L. *The Miracle of Theism*. Oxford: Clarendon, 1982.

Madsen, Truman. *Eternal Man*. Salt Lake City, UT: Deseret Books, 1966.

Martin, Walter R. *Kingdom of the Cults*. Revised Edition. Minneapolis: Bethany House, 1977.

Maxwell, Neal A. *All These Things Shall Give Thee Experience*. Salt Lake City, UT: Deseret Books, 1979.

McConkie, Bruce. *Mormon Doctrine*. 2nd edition. Salt Lake City, UT: Bookcraft, 1979.

McMurrin, Sterling. *The Philosophical Foundations of Mormon Theology*. Salt Lake City, UT: University of Utah Press, 1959.

_____. *The Theological Foundations of the Mormon Religion*. Salt Lake City, UT: University of Utah Press, 1965.

Melton, J. Gordon. *The Encyclopedia of American Religions*. 2nd edition. Detroit, MI: Gale Research Company, 1987.

_____. *The Encyclopedia of Cults in America*. New York: Garland, 1986.

Mill, John Stuart. *Nature, the Utility of Religion, and Theism*. London: Longmans, Green and Co., 1923.

Moreland, J.P. *Scaling the Secular City*. Grand Rapids, MI: Baker Book House, 1987.

_____. *Universals, Qualities, and Quality-Instances: A Defense of Realism*. Lanham, MD: University Press of America, 1985.

Morey, Robert A. *Battle of the Gods*. Southbridge, MA: Crown Publications, 1989.

Morris, Thomas V. *The Logic of God Incarnate*. Ithaca, NY: Cornell University Press, 1986.

Nash, Ronald H. *The Concept of God*. Grand Rapids, MI: Zondervan, 1983.

_____, ed. *Process Theology*. Grand Rapids, MI: Baker Book House, 1987.

Paulsen, David Lamont. *The Comparative Coherency of Mormon (Finitistic) and Classical Theism*. Ann Arbor, MI: University Microfilms, 1975.

Pinnock, Clark H., ed. *The Grace of God, The Will of Man*. Grand Rapids, MI: Zondervan/Academie, 1989.

Plantinga, Alvin. *Does God Have a Nature?* Milwaukee: Marquette University Press, 1980.

_____. *God, Freedom, and Evil*. Grand Rapids, MI: Eerdmans, 1974.

Plato. *The Collected Dialogues of Plato*. Edited by Edith Hamilton and Huntington Cairns. Princeton, NJ: Princeton University Press, 1961.

Purtill, Richard L. *Thinking About Religion: A Philosophical Introduction to Religion*. Englewood Cliffs, NJ: Prentice-Hall, 1978.

Ramm, Bernard. *Protestant Biblical Interpretation*. 3rd Revised Edition. Grand Rapids, MI: Baker Book House, 1970.

Rice, Richard. *God's Foreknowledge and Man's Free Will*. Minneapolis: Bethany House, 1985.

Roberts. B.H. *Seventy's Course in Theology: Third Year and Fourth Year*. Salt Lake City, UT: The Caxton Press, 1910.

Rowe, William L. *Philosophy of Religion*. Encino, CA: Dickenson, 1978.

Russell, Bertrand. *Why I Am Not a Christian*. New York: Simon & Schuster, 1957.

Sire, James. *Scripture Twisting*. Downers Grove, IL: InterVarsity Press, 1980.

Smith, Joseph Fielding. *Doctrines of Salvation*. 3 volumes. Salt Lake City, UT: Bookcraft, 1959.

Sorabji, Richard. *Time, Creation, and the Continuum*. Ithaca, NY: Cornell University Press, 1983.

Strong, Augustus Hopkins. *Systematic Theology: A Compendium*. Old Tappan, NJ: Fleming Revell, 1907.

Swinburne, Richard. *The Coherence of Theism*. Oxford: Clarendon, 1977.

_____. *The Evolution of the Soul*. Oxford: Clarendon, 1986.

Talmage, James E. *The Articles of Faith*. Salt Lake City, UT: Church of Jesus Christ of Latter-day Saints, 1957.

Taylor, Richard. *Metaphysics*. 2nd edition. Englewood Cliffs, NJ: Prentice-Hall, 1974.

Tucker, Bruce. *Twisting the Truth*. Minneapolis: Bethany House, 1987.

Tucker, Ruth A. *Another Gospel*. Grand Rapids, MI: Zondervan/Academie, 1989

Unger, Merrill F. and White, William, Jr., eds. *Nelson's Expository Dictionary of the Old Testament*. Nashville: Thomas Nelson, 1980.

White, O. Kendall. *Mormon Neo-Orthodoxy: A Crisis Theology*. Salt Lake City, UT: Signature Books, 1987.

Widtsoe, John A. *A Rational Theology*. Salt Lake City, UT: Deseret Books, 1915.

ARTICLES, PAPERS, AND REVIEWS

Alexander, Thomas G. "The Reconstruction of Mormon Doctrine: From Joseph Smith to Progressive Theology." *Sunstone* 5 (July-August 1980)

Allen, James B. "Emergence of a Fundamental: The Expanding Role of Joseph Smith's First Vision in Mormon Religious Thought." *Journal of Mormon History* 7 (1980)

Beckwith, Francis J. "Are Creationists Philosophically and Scientifically Justified in Postulating God?: A Critical Analysis of Naturalistic Evolution." *Interchange* (Australia) 46 (1989)

_____. "Baha'i-Christian Dialogue: Some Key Issues Considered." *Christian Research Journal* 11 (Winter/Spring, 1989)

_____. "Identity and Resurrection: A Review Article." *Journal of the Evangelical Theological Society* 33 (September 1990)

_____. "Of Logic and Lordship: The Validity of a Categorical Syllogism Suporting Christ's Deity." *Journal of the Evangelical Theological Society* 29 (December 1986)

_____. "The Mormon Concept of God: Two Philosophical Difficulties?" *Sunstone*, forthcoming

_____. review of *Signs and Wonders* by Norman L. Geisler and *The Third Wave of the Holy Spirit* by C. Peter Wagner. *Journal of the Evangelical Theological Society* 33 (September 1990)

_____. "Two Philosophical Problems with the Mormon Concept of God." Paper presented at the 40th annual meeting of the Evangelical Theological Society. Wheaton College. Wheaton, IL. 19 November 1988.

Beckwith, Francis J. and Parrish, Stephen E. "Mormon Theism and the Argument from Design." *Bulletin of the Evangelical Philosophical Society* 13 (1990)

_____. "The Mormon God, Omniscience, and Eternal Progression: A Philosophical Analysis." *Trinity Journal*, forthcoming.

_____. "Mormon Philosophical Apologetics: A Critique of Some Recent Arguments." Paper presented by Francis J. Beckwith at the 41st annual meeting of the Evangelical Theological Society. San Diego, CA. Bethel Theological Seminary West. 16 November 1989.

Bergera, Gary James. "The Orson Pratt-Brigham Young Controversies: Conflict Within the Quorums, 1853-1868." *Dialogue: A Journal of Mormon Thought* 13 (Summer 1980)

Bonansea, Bernardino. "The Impossibility of Creation from Eternity According to St. Bonaventure." *Proceedings of the American Catholic Philosophical Association* 48 (1974)

Bowman, Robert M., Jr. "How Mormons are Defending Their Faith." *Christian Research Journal* 11 (Fall 1988)

_____. "How Mormons are Defending Mormon Doctrine." *Christian Research Journal* 12 (Fall 1989)

Clarke, W. Norris. "A New Look at the Immutability of God." In *God, Knowable and Unknowable*, edited by Robert J. Roth. New York: Fordham University Press, 1973.

Craig, William Lane. "'No Other Name': A Middle Knowledge Perspective on the Exclusivity of Salvation Through Christ." *Faith and Philosophy* 6 (April 1989)

Edwards, Paul. "The Cosmological Argument." In *The Cosmological Arguments*, edited by Donald R. Burrill. New York: Doubleday, 1967.

Geisler, Norman L. "Process Theology." In *Tensions in Contemporary Theology*, edited by Stanley N. Gundry and Alan F. Johnson. Chicago: Moody Press, 1976.

Gomes, Alan. "God in Man's Image: Foreknowledge, Freedom, and the 'Openness' of God." *Christian Research Journal* 10 (Summer 1987)

Gott, J. Richard; Gunn, James E.; Schramm, David N.; and Tinsley, Beatrice M. "Will the Universe Expand Forever?" *Scientific American* (March 1976)

Grider J. Kenneth. "The Holy Trinity." In *Basic Christian Doctrines*. Edited by Carl F.H. Henry. New York: Holt, Rinehart and Winston, 1962.

Hale, Van. "Defining the Mormon Doctrine of Deity." *Sunstone* 10 (January 1985)

Hartshorne, Charles. "Alternative Conceptions of God." In *Religious Belief and Philosophical Thought*, edited by William A. Alston. New York: Harcourt, Brace and World, 1963.

_____. "Religion in Process-Philosophy." In *Religion in Philosophical and Cultural Perspective*. Edited by J. Clayton Feaver and William Horosz. Princeton, NJ: D. Van Norstrand, 1967.

Kaiser, Walter C., Jr. "Legitimate Hermeneutics." In *Inerrancy*, edited by Norman L. Geisler. Grand Rapids, MI: Zondervan, 1980.

Kenadjian, C. Glenn. "Is the Doctrine that God is Spirit Incoherent." *Journal of the Evangelical Theological Society* 31 (June 1988)

Kirkland, Boyd. "Elohim and Jehovah in Mormonism and the Bible." *Dialogue: A Journal of Mormon Thought* 19 (Spring 1986)

_____. "Jehovah as the Father." *Sunstone* 9 (Autumn 1984)

Layman, C. Stephen. "Tritheism and the Trinity" *Faith and Philosophy* 5 (July 1988)

Maxwell, Neal A. "A More Determined Discipleship." *Ensign* (February 1979)

McConkie, Bruce. "The Seven Deadly Heresies." Lecture Delivered at Brigham Young University. June 1, 1980.

Moreland, J.P. "The Emergent Property View of the Self and the Bundle Theory: A Development Without Substance." *Bulletin of the Evangelical Philosophical Society* 11 (1988)

Ostler, Blake. "The Idea of Pre-existence in the Development of Mormon Thought." *Dialogue: A Journal of Mormon Thought* 15 (Spring 1982)

_____. "The Mormon Concept of God." *Dialogue: A Journal of Mormon Thought* 17 (Summer 1984)

Paulsen, David. "Must God Be Incorporeal?" *Faith and Philosophy* 6 (January 1989)

Robson, Kent. "Omnis on the Horizon." *Sunstone* 8 (July-August 1983)

_____. "Time and Omniscience in Mormon Theology." *Sunstone* 5 (May-June 1980)

Rowe, William L. "Two Criticisms of the Cosmological Argument." In *Logical Analysis and Contemporary Theism*, edited by John Donnelly. New York: Fordham University Press, 1972.

Russell, Bertrand and Copleston, F.C. "A Debate on the Existence of God." In *The Existence of God*, edited by John Hick. New York: Macmillan, 1964.

Sadowsky, James. review of *The Kalam Cosmological Argument* by William Lane Craig. *International Philosophical Quarterly* 21 (June 1981)

Salmon, Wesley C. "Religion and Science: A New Look at Hume's Dia-
    logues." *Philosophical Studies* 33 (1978)

Swiburne, Richard. "Could There Be More Than One God?" *Faith and
    Philosophy* 5 (July 1988)

Tingle, Donald S. "Latter-day Saints (Mormons)." In *A Guide to Cults and
    New Religions*. Edited by Ronald Enroth. Downers Grove, IL: In-
    terVarsity Press, 1983.

Wainwright, William. review of *The Kalam Cosmological Argument* by Wil-
    liam Lane Craig. *Nous* 16 (May 1982).

Wolterstorff, Nicholas. "God Everlasting." In *God and the Good*, edited by
    Clifton Orlebeke and Lewis Smedes. Grand Rapids, MI: Eerdmans,
    1975.

THESES AND DISSERTATIONS

Parrish, Stephen E. "Finitistic Theism and Teleology." M.A. Thesis. Wayne
    State University. Detroit, MI. 1984.

_____. "Necessary Being and the Theistic Arguments." Ph.D.
    Dissertation. Wayne State University. Detroit, MI. 1991.

Watkins, William D. "The Dipolar God of Charles Hartshorne: A Classical
    Theist's Examination." Th.M. Thesis. Dallas Theological Seminary.
    Dallas, TX. 1983.

LATTER-DAY SAINT SCRIPTURE AND HISTORICAL WORKS

Book of Mormon. Translated by Joseph Smith. Salt Lake City, UT: The
    Church of Jesus Christ of Latter-day Saints, 1971.

*The Doctrine and Covenants of the Church of Jesus Christ of Latter-day
    Saints*. Salt Lake City, UT: The Church of Jesus Christ of Latter-day
    Saints, 1971.

*Journal of Discourses, by Brigham Young, President of the Church of Jesus
    Christ of Latter-day Saints, His Two Counsellors, the Twelve Apostles,
    and Others*. 26 volumes. Reported by G.D. Watt. Liverpool: F.D.
    Richards, 1854-1886.

Pearl of Great Price. Translated by Joseph Smith. Salt Lake City, UT: The
    Church of Jesus Christ of Latter-day Saints, 1971.

Smith, Joseph. *History of the Church of Jesus Christ of Latter-day Saints*. 7 volumes. Introduction and Notes by B.H. Roberts. 2nd edition revised. Salt Lake City, UT: The Deseret Book Company, 1978.

*Indicates officially canonized Mormon Scripture which the LDS church claims is as divinely inspired as the Christian Bible.

INDEX

STUDIES IN AMERICAN RELIGION

22. Stafford Poole and Douglas J. Slawson, **Church And Slave in Perry County, Missouri, 1818-1865**

23. Rebecca Moore, **The Jonestown Letters: Correspondence of the Moore Family 1970-1985**

24. Lawrence H. Williams, **Black Higher Education in Kentucky 1879-1930: The History of Simmons University**

25. Erling Jorstad, **The New Christian Right, 1981- 1988: Prospects for the Post-Reagan Decade**

26. Joseph H. Hall, **Presbyterian Conflict and Resolution on the Missouri Frontier**

27. Jonathan Wells, **Charles Hodges' Critique of Darwinism: An Historical-Critical Analysis of Concepts Basic to the 19th Century Debate**

28. Donald R. Tuck, **Buddhist Churches of America: Jodo Shinshu**

29. Suzanne Geissler, **Lutheranism and Anglicanism in Colonial New Jersey: An Early Ecumenical Experiment in New Sweden**

30. David Hein, **A Student's View of The College of St. James on the Eve of the Civil War: The Letters of W. Wilkins Davis (1842-1866)**

31. Char Miller, **Selected Writings of Hiram Bingham (1814-1869), Missionary To The Hawaiian Islands: To Raise the Lord's Banner**

32. Rebecca Moore, **In Defense of Peoples Temple-And Other Essays**

33. Donald L. Huber, **Educating Lutheran Pastors in Ohio, 1830-1980: A History of Trinity Lutheran Seminary and its Predecessors**

34. Hugh Spurgin, **Roger Williams and Puritan Radicalism in the English Separatist Tradition**

35. Michael Meiers, **Was Jonestown A CIA Medical Experiment?: A Review of the Evidence**

36. L. Raymond Camp, **Roger Williams, God's Apostle of Advocacy: Biography and Rhetoric**

37. Rebecca Moore & Fielding M. McGehee III (eds.), **New Religious Movements, Mass Suicide, and Peoples Temple: Scholarly Perspectives on a Tragedy**

38. Annabelle S. Wenzke, **Timothy Dwight (1752-1817)**

39. Joseph R. Washington, Jr., **Race and Religion in Early Nineteenth Century America 1800-1850: Constitution, Conscience, and Calvinist Compromise** (2 vols.)

40. Joseph R. Washington, Jr., **Race and Religion in Mid-Nineteenth Century America 1850-1877: Protestant Parochial Philanthropists** (2 vols.)

41. Rebecca Moore & Fielding M. McGehee III (eds.), **The Need for a Second Look at Jonestown**

42. Joel Fetzer, **Selective Prosecution of Religiously Motivated Offenders in America: Scrutinizing the Myth of Neutrality**

43. Charles H. Lippy, **The Christadelphians in North America**